Personal Best

B1+ Intermediate

Student's Book and Workbook combined edition **A**

Series Editor
Jim Scrivener

Student's Book Author
Graham Burton

Workbook Authors
Elizabeth Walter
and **Kate Woodford**

Richmond

STUDENT'S BOOK CONTENTS

Language App, unit-by-unit grammar and vocabulary games

Communication

1A Connected

1 How do you keep in touch with people? Order the communication phrases from 1 (I do this less often) to 6 (I do this most often). Compare your answers in pairs.

☐ get a text message ☐ share a photo ☐ give someone a call ☐ reply to an e-mail ☐ check your phone ☐ comment on a post

Personal Best

Go to Vocabulary practice: communication, page 136

2 Think of three people in your life. Tell your partner how you keep in touch with these people.

3 A Are sentences 1–6 true (T) or false (F)? Discuss your answers in pairs.

1 We speak to each other face-to-face more often nowadays. _____
2 Our phone calls are longer today compared to ten years ago. _____
3 These days, it seems we prefer text messages to phone calls. _____
4 People in the U.S. send more letters and packages nowadays. _____
5 We are sending a million e-mails per second, now. _____
6 More than half of the Internet pages we visit are social media sites. _____

B Read the text and check your answers in 3A. Correct the false sentences.

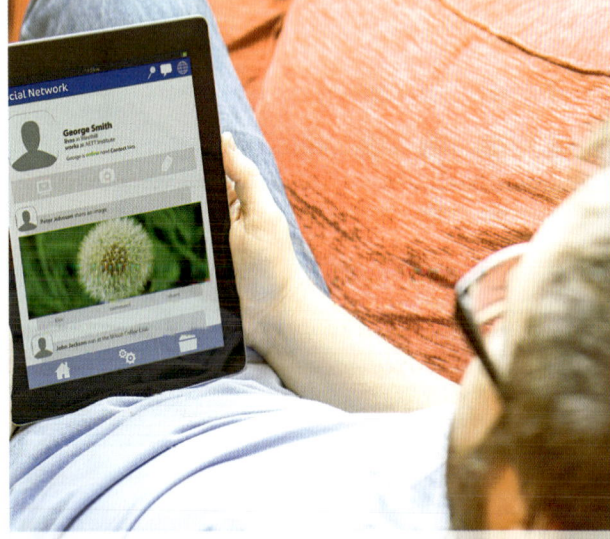

We talk to each other less.

Ten years ago, 80% of our communication was face-to-face. Now, it's only 60%. Even our phone calls are shorter – on average, each call now lasts one minute, compared to three minutes ten years ago. It seems that people prefer texting to calling.

We use traditional postal services less.

In the U.S., over 200 billion letters and packages were sent in 2008, compared to 150 billion last year. These days, we usually write to people by text, messaging app, or e-mail. In fact, right now, people are sending two million e-mails per second!

We love social media.

Sixty percent of the pages we view on the Internet are social media pages, and we share nearly two billion photos on them every day. The average person has five social media accounts and spends about two hours a day looking at them.

THE CHANGING FACE OF COMMUNICATION

The way we communicate has never changed so much in such a short period of time. We look at the results of recent surveys that tell us about the changing face of communication.

Comments

Tina

It's a shame we *don't write* letters much, but the post office *seems* so slow nowadays compared to communicating online! I *need* the Internet to be in immediate contact with people, especially right now because I'*m planning* my wedding.

Rob

I agree with Tina, but I still try to send letters and cards on important occasions, and postcards when I'm on vacation. I don't know how people planned things with just snail mail!

4 Which piece of information in the text did you find most surprising? Do you agree with Tina and Rob?

5 **A** Look at the highlighted verbs in Tina's comment and answer the questions.

1 Which four verbs are in the simple present? Which verb is in the present continuous?
2 Which two verbs describe actions? Which three verbs describe states?

B Choose the correct options to complete the rules

1 We use the *simple present / present continuous* to talk about things that happen regularly or things that are always true.
2 We use the *simple present / present continuous* to talk about actions that are happening now or actions that are temporary.
3 We can't use the present continuous for *action / state* verbs.

6 Read the Grammar box. Then look at the sentences in exercise 3A again. Do they contain action or state verbs? What tense are they?

📖 **Grammar**   **simple present and present continuous; action and state verbs**

Simple present with action and state verbs:
*I **call** my brother at least once a week.*   *I'm so thirsty right now. I **need** some water.* NOT ~~I'm needing some water~~.

Present continuous with action verbs:
*I**'m calling** you from New York!*   *We**'re studying** French this year.*

Personal Best

Go to Grammar practice: simple present and present continuous; action and state verbs, page 112

7 **A** ▶1.3 **Pronunciation:** sentence stress Listen to the sentences. Do we stress the auxiliary verbs *be* and *do*?

1 Are you trying to access the Internet?
2 Do you need a new laptop?
3 The Internet doesn't seem slow right now.
4 Why are you using my tablet?

B ▶1.3 Listen, check, and repeat.

8 **A** Complete the sentences with the correct tense of the verbs in parentheses.

1 I _____ (not check) my text messages when I'm having coffee with friends.
2 The price of desktop computers _____ (go) down at the moment.
3 I _____ (like) looking at the selfie photos that my friends post on social media.
4 I'm studying English online, right now, so I _____ (need) the Internet on my phone.
5 I _____ (look) for a new phone because my phone is very old.
6 Most people _____ (have) friends on Facebook that they never talk to face-to-face.

B In pairs, discuss the sentences in 8A. Which sentences do you agree with or are true for you?

Go to Communication practice: Student A page 156, Student B page 166

9 Complete the questionnaire and discuss your answers in pairs.

How do you communicate?

1 When I want to get together with friends, I normally …
message them on Facebook. ☐   text them. ☐
call them. ☐

2 When I'm feeling happy and I want to share good news with people that live far away, I …
send a text message. ☐   send a letter. ☐
make plans to get together. ☐

3 When I'm feeling sad, I prefer to speak to people …
on the phone. ☐   on Skype. ☐   face-to-face. ☐

4 On my best friend's birthday, I usually send …
a message on social media. ☐   a text. ☐   a card. ☐

5 I usually share important photos …
using a messaging app. ☐   by e-mail. ☐
on social media. ☐

6 When I want to keep in touch with old friends, I usually …
contact them on social media. ☐   e-mail them. ☐
give them a call. ☐

Personal Best   Write four sentences with state verbs in the simple present.

5

1B Smart living?

1 What do you use your smartphone for? What do you think of people who constantly check their phones?

🔧 **Skill** skimming a text

Before you read a text in detail, get a general idea of the topic of the text and of each paragraph.
- Read the title of the text and look at any images. Can you predict what the text is about?
- Quickly read the first paragraph. This will confirm the topic and can give you an idea of the text content and organization.
- Read the first sentence of each paragraph. This can give you information about the main idea of each paragraph.

2 Read the Skill box. Then look at the title of the text, the picture, and the first paragraph on page 7. Do you think the writer had a positive or negative experience without his smartphone?

3 Read the first sentences of paragraphs 2–6. What is the main idea of each paragraph? Match the paragraphs with ideas a–e.

  a With no smartphone, he felt less tired.
  b He worked better.
  c He communicated more often face-to-face.
  d There were more advantages than disadvantages.
  e He found things to do to entertain himself.

4 Read the complete text. Are the sentences true (T) or false (F)? Correct the false sentences.

  1 The writer stopped using his smartphone because of an article he read. _____
  2 Normally his smartphone distracts him when he's working. _____
  3 He has become a better listener when he's with friends. _____
  4 He doesn't enjoy reading books and newspapers any more. _____
  5 The light from smartphone screens helps us sleep. _____
  6 The writer now uses his smartphone differently than before. _____

5 Read this sentence from the text. Which word is used to express surprise that something unexpected happened?

"I actually talked to people more and felt more connected to them, although we weren't in constant contact online."

🧩 **Text builder** *actually, in fact*

To say that something is surprising or unexpected, we can use *actually* or *in fact*:
*I was worried that I would be bored without my phone as entertainment, but, **actually**, I enjoyed it.*
*I thought living without a smartphone would be hard, but, **in fact**, it was pretty easy.*

Look! We can use ***actually*** at the start of a phrase, before a main verb, or after *be*.
We usually use ***in fact*** at the start of a phrase.

6 Read the Text builder. Match 1–4 with a–d.

  1 My friends say I'm addicted to my new smartphone.
  2 My teacher's surprised because
  3 Tim thought the movie was on at 8:30 this evening,
  4 I thought I was going away this weekend,

  a but it was actually on yesterday, not today.
  b Actually, I don't use it as much as my old one.
  c but, in fact, I'm staying at home.
  d I actually passed the exam!

7 Could you live without your smartphone for a week? In pairs, discuss what you think the experience would be like.

A WEEK WITHOUT MY
smartphone

by David Sharpe

1 When I read that we spend three hours every day checking our smartphones, I was surprised. What was I missing in the real world when walking down the street, lost in a virtual world of social media updates and videos of dogs on bicycles? I promised myself I would use my smartphone less … but it didn't happen. But then my phone died, and I had to wait a week for a new one. Would I survive? I thought it would be hard, but, in fact, it was pretty easy – and surprising, in a good way, for a number of reasons!

2 The first result was pretty amazing – on the first day in the office without my phone, I was thinking more deeply and concentrating more. I had rediscovered my brain! Not having access to my favorite apps meant that I wasn't interrupted every five minutes by social media alerts, soccer scores, and WhatsApp group messages. Without these distractions, I was more productive and felt satisfied that I'd done a better job.

3 Another result was that I actually talked to people more and felt more connected to them, although we weren't in constant contact online. At lunch with friends one day, I realized I was being more responsive to their news and sympathetic to their problems because I wasn't constantly checking my phone. Another day I was in a new city and I asked people for directions instead of using an app. Their kindness made me feel welcome, and I discovered my brain has a very good GPS!

4 I was worried that I would be bored without my phone as entertainment, but, actually, I enjoyed it – I'd forgotten how much I love books and newspapers. I'd also forgotten how much I enjoyed doing Sudoku puzzles. I had an app for that on my smartphone, but never used it. Doing one every day in the newspaper felt a lot more special, and it became part of my morning routine. My brain felt a lot sharper and much more ready for the day ahead as a result.

5 One completely unexpected result of not having a smartphone was that I slept so much better and felt more awake in the morning. At night, I relaxed with a book before going to sleep, instead of watching Netflix or reading the news on my phone. Apparently, the blue light from smartphone screens makes our brain think it's morning, so it's releasing chemicals to wake us up, just when we're trying to get to sleep. That's not very smart!

6 Of course, at times, it was extremely inconvenient to have no cell-phone Internet connection, but, all in all, there were a lot of benefits to not being connected 24/7. Although I was jumping for joy when my new smartphone arrived, I'm a lot more careful about how much I use it now. So, if you think you use your smartphone too much, put it away for a few days and see what happens. You never know, you may become smarter!

1C Liar, liar

1 In pairs, answer the questions.

   1 What are the people in the pictures lying about?

   2 What other things do people often tell lies about? Make a list.

a

b

c

d

Go to Vocabulary practice: *say*, *tell*, *speak*, and *talk*, page 136

2 A In pairs, take the quiz "The truth about lying."

THE TRUTH ABOUT LYING

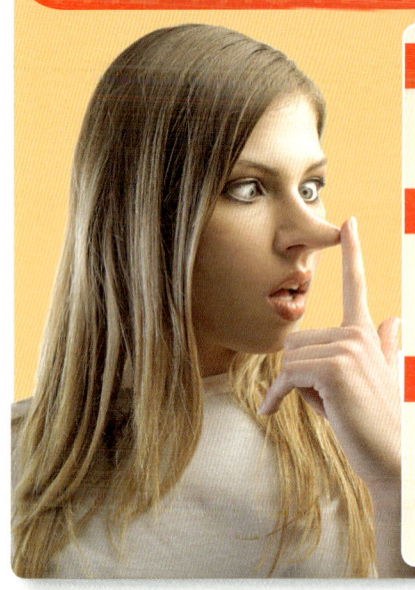

1 How often do people tell lies?
  a twice a month
  b twice a week
  c twice a day

2 What do people lie about most frequently?
  a work
  b money
  c unimportant things

3 How do people usually answer the question, "When did you last tell a lie?"
  a "I never lie."
  b "I can't remember."
  c "Some time today."

4 How can you know when people are lying?
  a They don't look directly at you.
  b They move their hands a lot.
  c They give unnecessary information.

5 Is communication technology making us less honest?
  a yes   **b** no

6 Do men lie more often than women?
  a yes   **b** no

7 Do men and women lie about the same things?
  a yes   **b** no

B ▶ 1.5 Listen and check your answers. Which answer surprised you most?

3 Cover the quiz. Complete the questions from memory. Then check your answers in the quiz.

  1 _____ lies?

  2 _____ most frequently?

  3 _____ last _____ a lie?

  4 _____ when people are lying?

  5 _____ us less honest?

4 A Look at questions 1–5 in exercise 3. How do we form most questions? Choose the correct structure, a or b.

  a (question word/s) + auxiliary verb + subject + main verb

  b (question word/s) + main verb

  B Look at question 2 in exercise 3. Is the preposition before the question word or after the main verb?

5 **A** ▶1.6   Listen to people telling a lie in three conversations. What is each person lying about? Write the conversation number (1–3).

a receiving text messages _____   **b** eating chocolate _____   **c** liking someone's food _____

B ▶1.6   Listen again and complete the questions.

1 Who _____ all of my chocolate?   **3** Who _____ more banana and potato sandwiches?

2 What _____ to you last night?

6 Look at the questions in exercise 5B. Choose the correct options to complete the sentences. Then read the Grammar box about the different question forms.

1 In these questions, we *know / don't know* the subject of the verb.

2 We use the *affirmative / question* form of the verb.

Grammar | **question forms**

Object questions:
Where do you work?
What are you doing right now?
Where did you go to college?
Have you finished?

Questions with prepositions:
*Where do they come **from**?*
*Who did you play tennis **with**?*

Subject questions:
Who called me? NOT ~~Who did call me?~~
Who wants coffee? NOT ~~Who does want coffee?~~
Who invented the telephone? NOT ~~Who did invent the telephone?~~

Go to Grammar practice: question forms, page 113

7 ▶1.8   **Pronunciation:** question intonation Listen to four of the questions from this lesson. Does the intonation go up (↗) or down (↘) at the end of the questions?

1 Have you finished?   **3** What happened to you last night?

2 How often do people tell lies?   **4** Do men lie more often than women?

8 **A** Complete the questions with an auxiliary verb from the box if necessary. Which question doesn't need an auxiliary?

> do (x2) did (x5) have

1 _____ you usually tell little white lies to protect people's feelings?

2 When _____ you last tell a little white lie? What _____ you lie about?

3 When you were younger, _____ you tell your parents lies? _____ you tell the truth later?

4 Who _____ tells the best jokes in your family?

5 _____ you usually say hello to people you don't know on the street?

6 _____ you ever told someone that he or she can't cook well? What _____ the person say?

B In pairs, decide if the intonation goes up (↗) or down (↘) at the end of the questions in 8A. Then ask and answer the questions.

Go to Communication practice: Student A page 156, Student B page 166

9 Ask and answer the questions in pairs.

1 Who helped you with your homework as a child?

2 Who taught you how to ride a bike?

3 What happened on your first day of school?

4 Who taught you how to drive?

5 Which author wrote your favorite book?

6 What happened on your first day at work?

Personal Best Write four questions to ask your partner about his or her life.

Learning Curve

1D Small talk

1 A Read the definition of *small talk* and look at the topics. Which topics do people typically discuss when they make small talk?

> **small talk** *noun* polite and informal conversation about light topics, often between people who don't know each other well.

the weather

politics

TV, sports, and movies

relationship problems

work and family

the situation (party, trip, etc.)

your day

B In pairs, discuss the questions.

1 When did you last make small talk?
2 Where were you?
3 Who did you talk to?
4 What did you talk about?

2 ▶1.9 Watch or listen to the first part of a webshow called *Learning Curve*. Ethan catches a train, and a passenger makes small talk with him. Who are sentences 1–6 about? Check (✓) *Ethan* or *passenger*.

	Ethan	passenger
1 He starts the conversation.	☐	☐
2 He asks where the other person is going.	☐	☐
3 He's going to City Island.	☐	☐
4 He asks where the other person is from.	☐	☐
5 He's from Pennsylvania.	☐	☐
6 He asks about the other person's job.	☐	☐

3 ▶1.9 Complete the sentences from the conversation with the words in the box. Watch or listen again and check.

> so   nice   mind   ahead   have   excuse   sounds   living

1 _____ me. Does this train go to the baseball stadium?
2 Would you _____ if I sit here?
3 Uh, no. Go right _____.
4 _____, where are you going?
5 What do you do for a _____?
6 Well, that _____ interesting.
7 Hey, it was _____ talking to you!
8 _____ fun at the game!

Conversation builder   making small talk

Starting the conversation
Excuse me ...
Is anyone sitting here?
Would you mind if I sit here?
Beautiful day, isn't it?

Asking about the person/situation
Are you having a good time/trip/day?
Are you from around here?
So, what do you do for a living?
And what does that involve?
I love your phone. Is it new?

Ending the conversation
Nice talking to you.
Great to meet you.
Have a nice evening.

4 Read the Conversation builder. Make small talk with your partner. Imagine it's your first English class and you've never met.

5 ▶ 1.10   Watch or listen to the second part of the show. Ethan goes to a party and meets Cindy for the first time. Check (✔) the topics that Cindy and Ethan talk about.

1 Penny and Taylor's apartment ☐
2 their families ☐
3 their jobs ☐
4 how they know Penny and Taylor ☐
5 the food at the party ☐
6 the weather ☐

6 ▶ 1.10   Put sentences (a–I) in order. Watch or listen again and check.

a ☐ **Cindy** So, what do you do on your webshow?

b ☐ **Ethan** Oh, you met at work! So, are you having a good time?

c ☐ **Cindy** Sorry, I don't know Penny that well. By the way, I'm Cindy. I work with Taylor at the gym.

d ☐ **Ethan** Well, I'm a presenter, a co-host, like Penny.

e ☐ 1 **Cindy** How do you know Penny and Taylor?

f ☐ **Ethan** Mmm! Well, I love carrot cake.

g ☐ **Cindy** It's a great party. I got here early so I could bring my famous carrot cake.

h ☐ 2 **Ethan** I'm Ethan. I work with Penny on *Learning Curve*. It's a webshow. We're presenters.

I ☐ **Cindy** Hmm, a presenter, that's interesting. And what does that involve?

🔧 **Skill**   **keeping a conversation going**

When we talk to someone we don't know well, we keep the conversation going so we don't run out of things to say.

- Give extra information when you answer a question, e.g., *"Are you from around here?" "No. I moved here from Brazil six months ago."*
- Respond to a statement with a positive comment, e.g., *"That's interesting! I love Brazil. I've been there twice."*
- Ask open questions to find out more information, e.g., *"Really? What were you doing there?"*

---

7 Read the Skill box. Answer the questions about the conversation in exercise 6.

1 What extra information does Ethan give when he explains how he knows Penny?
2 What positive comments do Ethan and Cindy make?
3 What open questions does Cindy ask?

8 In pairs, practice the conversation in exercise 6.

Go to Communication practice: Student A page 156, Student B page 166

9 **A** **PREPARE** In pairs, choose one of the situations below and think about how you could start a conversation with someone you don't know well.

B **PRACTICE** Take turns starting a conversation. Make small talk and keep the conversation going.

C **PERSONAL BEST** Was it easy to start the conversation and keep it going? What could you do differently next time? Choose another situation and have another conversation.

Personal Best   You meet someone new at Penny and Taylor's party. Write the conversation.

Tell me a story

2A What a coincidence!

1 A Choose the correct options to complete the questions. Explain why they are correct.

    1 In your opinion, what kind of social media posts are *bored* / *boring*?

    2 What kind of social media posts are you *interested* / *interesting* in?

B In pairs, answer the questions in 1A.

Go to Vocabulary practice: *-ed* and *-ing* adjectives, page 137

2 Tell your partner about the last time you felt shocked or terrified, and about something you find fascinating or amusing.

3 A Read the text quickly. What do you think the title *Twinsters* means?

B Read the text again. Order the events from 1–6.

a ☐ The twins made a movie about finding each other.

b ☐ Anaïs saw a woman online who looked identical to her.

c ☐ Anaïs found a way of contacting Samantha.

d ☐ Anaïs discovered that they had the same date of birth.

e ☐ They got to know each other online, and then they met in person.

f ☐ A scientific test proved they were twins.

In February 2013, 25-year-old Anaïs Bordier, a fashion design student from Paris, was checking Facebook when she saw a video of a young American actress that a friend had posted. Anaïs couldn't believe it – the actress looked exactly like her! Unfortunately, there was no name on the video, but she was extremely curious and told all her friends about it.

A few months later, while Anaïs was traveling by bus to college, she got a message from the same friend. He had seen the actress in another video, and this time there was a name – Samantha Futerman. When Anaïs googled her, she found out that they were born on the same day, and that, like Anaïs, Samantha had been adopted when she was a baby. Anaïs was so shocked that she got off the bus. Could Samantha be her twin? She decided to contact her to find out.

When Samantha received a friend request from Anaïs on Facebook, she was amazed to see that the face in the profile picture was identical to her own. Anaïs messaged Samantha to explain how she had found her, and to ask her where she was born. Samantha replied and confirmed that she was also born in Busan, South Korea. The girls spoke regularly on Skype after that and discovered that they were not only very similar in appearance, but also had the same mannerisms, found the same things amusing, and both loved cheese!

Anaïs and Samantha were excited to meet for the first time several months later in London, where Anaïs was studying. While Samantha was visiting Anaïs, they received the results of a DNA test which confirmed what they already knew – that they really were identical twins. The sisters then wrote a book and filmed an award-winning documentary, *Twinsters*, about their amazing story.

4 What did you think of Anaïs and Samantha's story?

I thought it was an amazing coincidence.

5 **A** Which forms are the verbs in **bold**? Choose from the simple past, past perfect, and past continuous.

1 He **had seen** the actress in another video.

2 While Anaïs **was traveling** by bus to college, she got a message. _____

3 The sisters **wrote** a book about their amazing story. _____

B Match the forms with their uses. Then read the Grammar box.

a an action that happened before another action in the past _____

b a completed action in the past _____

c an action in progress at a specific moment in the past _____

📖 **Grammar** narrative tenses

Simple past (for main events):	Past perfect (for actions that happened before other actions):	Past continuous (for longer actions/ background):
*I **visited** my friend Ana last year.*	*When we arrived at the theater, the movie **had started**.*	*At 9 p.m. last night I **was having** dinner.*

Look! We usually use **when** with the simple past and **when** or **while** with the past continuous:
*I was walking in the park **when** I met Jo.*   **When/While** *I was walking in the park, I met Jo.*

Go to Grammar practice: narrative tenses, page 114

6 **A** ▶2.3 **Pronunciation:** /d/ in the past perfect Listen to the sentence. Notice the pronunciation of /d/ in the past perfect form. Listen again and repeat.

He**'d** seen the woman before.

B ▶2.4 Listen to the sentences and choose the verb forms you hear.

1 *I bought / I'd bought*   3 *She caught the bus / She'd caught the bus*   5 *You watched / You'd watched*

2 *He asked / He'd asked*   4 *We realized / We'd realized*   6 *They lost / They'd lost*

Go to Communication practice: Student A page 157, Student B page 167

7 **A** ▶2.5 Complete the text with the correct form of the verbs in parentheses. Listen and check.

Last year, while I ¹_____ (stay) with my grandmother for the weekend in a town a few hours away, I ²_____ (go) to visit my friend Marco, who also lives there. I ³_____ (call) him the day before to arrange a time to get together, but he hadn't answered. I went to his house anyway, but when I ⁴_____ (ring) the doorbell, nobody ⁵_____ (come) to the door, so I ⁶_____ (decide) to leave. Right then, I ⁷_____ (get) a message on my phone. It was Marco! He ⁸_____ (go) to my hometown the evening before to visit his parents, and now he ⁹_____ (knock) on my door! It was such a coincidence!

B Have there been any coincidences in your life or in your friends' lives? Talk about them in pairs.

8 In pairs, talk about a time when you met someone important in your life. Use the questions to help you.

- *Where were you?*
- *What had happened before you met?*
- *What were you both doing when you met?*
- *What happened when you met?*
- *What did you both say?*
- *How did your life change after you met him/her?*

Personal Best Read the story about Anaïs and Samantha again. Close your books and retell the story in pairs.

2B Do we make our own luck?

1 Do you think these things bring good or bad luck? Can you think of more examples?

a dream catcher

a broken mirror

a fortune cat

a penny

13
the number 13

a four-leaf clover

2 A Were these people lucky or unlucky? Match the verbs in **bold** with the meanings.

> I found a lucky penny on the street, but that day, my car ¹**ran out** of gas and my boyfriend ²**broke up** with me – we'd been ³**going out** for ten years. So much for lucky pennies!

> My plane ticket was for seat 13. I ⁴**set off** early for the airport to get there on time, but the traffic was terrible, and I ⁵**ended up** missing my flight. I was really ⁶**looking forward to** that vacation!

a be excited about something in the future
b finally be in a situation or place you didn't originally intend
c have a romantic relationship
d start a trip
e finish or use all of something
f end a relationship

B Answer the questions in pairs.

1 Has the battery on your phone ever run out right before an important call?
2 What did you plan to do last weekend? Did you end up doing something different?
3 What are you looking forward to right now?

Go to Vocabulary practice: phrasal verbs, page 138

🔧 **Skill**   **listening for the main idea**

It's important to understand the main idea when someone is speaking.
- Think about who is speaking and what the topic is.
- Remember that speakers often repeat the main idea using different words.
- Listen for key words, which are often stressed.
- Don't worry if you don't understand all the words or details.

3 A ▶2.8 Read the Skill box. Watch or listen to the first part of *Learning Curve* and choose the correct option to answer the questions.

1 What does Penny talk about?
a a scientific experiment about luck
b a book about luck
c an unlucky day she had
2 What is the main idea?
a Some people are simply unlucky.
b Positive people generally see more opportunities in life.
c People who believe they are lucky are usually unlucky.

Learning C

B Do you believe in luck? Do you think people make their own luck? Discuss in pairs.

4 ▶ **2.9** Watch or listen to the second part of the show. Complete the sentences about the main ideas with *Herman*, *Winnie*, or *Juan*.

1 _____ considers himself/herself to be very lucky.
2 _____ talks about someone else who believes in bad luck.
3 _____ is having a bit of bad luck, but his/her luck changes.

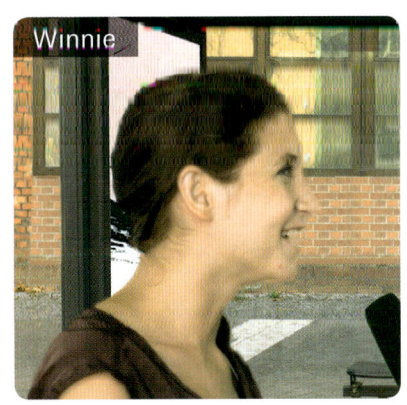

5 ▶ **2.9** Watch or listen again. Choose the correct option to answer the questions.

1 What happened to Herman earlier?
  a He slept badly, lost his keys, and left for work late.
  b His motorcycle broke down, he lost his keys, and missed the bus.
  c The shower ran out of hot water, and he lost his key chain.
2 What happened to Winnie?
  a She went out with a dentist and ended up marrying him.
  b She was going out with a mechanic, but broke up with him.
  c She ended up marrying a man she'd met several times by chance.
3 Which sentence about Juan is true?
  a He's looking forward to getting married to Winnie.
  b He's in the city doing a favor for a neighbor.
  c He has to go back home because he forgot his backpack.

6 Think of a time when you were lucky or unlucky. Describe what happened in pairs.

🧩 **Listening builder** | **linking consonants and vowels**

When a word ends in a consonant sound, we often move the consonant sound to the beginning of the next word if it starts with a vowel sound. This can sometimes mean it's difficult to hear the correct words.

It all started last night.   She's trying on her wedding dress.

---

7 ▶ **2.10** Read the Listening builder. Look at the sentences from the show and mark where the consonant-vowel links are. Listen and check. Then practice saying the sentences.

1 Do we make our own luck?
2 I ran out of energy.
3 I think Ethan is back.
4 I'm picking up a package.
5 I think it's his backpack.
6 I'm the luckiest person I know.

8 Discuss the questions in pairs.

1 Who's the luckiest person you know? And the unluckiest?
2 Do you have any lucky charms? What are they? Have they brought you good luck?
3 Is there anything you avoid doing because it might bring bad luck?

Personal Best | Write a paragraph about things that bring good luck on special occasions, e.g., a wedding, New Year's Eve.

2C Radical changes

1 **A** In pairs, look at the pictures and describe what you see. What are the similarities and differences?

B Read the text and choose the best caption for the pictures.

1 Steve Way and his trainer   **2** Steve Way: before and after   **3** Like father, like son

Sports interview:

Marathon Man

Steve Way, a long-distance runner, has two memorable career highlights: running a marathon in Glasgow in just 2 hours and 15 minutes and finishing the British Ultramarathon (100 km.) in 6 hours and 19 minutes. Both were personal best times for him and broke records. He is a top athlete, but behind the success there is an extraordinary story.

Steve usually runs about 120 km. a week, weighs 67 kg., and like all top athletes, is normally very careful about what he eats. But he hasn't always been so healthy. When Steve was in his thirties, he used to be dangerously overweight because of his addiction to chocolate and junk food. He didn't use to get any exercise, smoked a pack of cigarettes a day, and had a stressful job with long hours.

He felt horrible, "I could hardly sleep at night. I was coughing and waking up because of the smoking," he remembers. "I realized I had to do something radically different to break the cycle." The radical change was to give up smoking and start training for the London Marathon, which he completed in just over three hours despite training for only three weeks!

It soon became clear that Steve was a very talented athlete. Nowadays, he is so enthusiastic about running that he travels to competitions all over the world. So how does an ultra-healthy person celebrate another successful marathon? Steve admits that for 48 hours after a marathon he usually lets the old Steve out of the box and enjoys fast food, steak, and French fries. "I still struggle to see myself as a serious athlete," he says. "I am just a man who got obsessed with his hobby."

Adapted from theguardian.com

2 Read the text again. What do the numbers refer to?

> 100 km. 6 hours 19 minutes thirties three weeks 48 hours

3 In pairs, complete the notes about Steve in the chart with the words in the box.

> overweight healthy food 67 kg. runs a lot junk food get any exercise

	now	before
amount of exercise	1 He usually _____ .	2 He didn't use to _____ .
weight	3 He weighs _____ .	4 He used to be _____ .
diet	5 He usually eats _____ .	6 He used to eat _____ .

4 Have you made any changes in your life? What changes would you like to make?

5 Answer the questions and then read the Grammar box. Which sentences in the chart in exercise 3 describe:

1 present habits and states? _____ _____ _____
2 past habits and states? _____ _____ _____

📖 **Grammar** *used to* and *usually*

Past habits and states:
I used to be in shape.
I didn't use to work.
He never used to call me.
Did you use to do your homework?

Present habits:
I usually walk to work,
I don't usually watch much TV
Do you usually start work so early?

Look! We use the simple past for things that happened only once, or to say how many times something happened.
I broke my leg three times when I was a child. NOT ~~I used to break my leg three times.~~

Go to Grammar practice: *used to* and *usually*, page 115

6 ▶ 2.12 **Pronunciation:** sentence stress Read sentences 1–3. Which syllables are stressed? Listen, check, and repeat.

1 Did they use to play sports?   2 I used to go to the gym.   3 He didn't use to run.

7 A Rewrite the sentences with *usually* or a form of *used to*.

1 These days, I have cereal for breakfast.
2 I didn't play volleyball when I was younger.
3 I enjoyed math when I was in school.
4 I go swimming on Saturdays.
5 I ate healthier food as a teenager.
6 I didn't like fruit when I was young.
7 I don't eat much fast food.
8 I didn't work hard in school.

B Which of the sentences in 7A are true for you? Change the other sentences so they are true for you. Discuss your answers in pairs.

Go to Communication practice: Student A page 157, Student B page 167

8 A Use the prompts to make questions with the correct form of *used to*.

1 which TV shows / watch / when you were eight?
_____

2 which candies and snacks / like / when you were young?
_____

3 which toys / play with / when you were a child?
_____

4 which sports / play / in school?
_____

5 where / go on vacation / when you were a child?
_____

6 have / pet / when you were young?
_____

7 which pop group / like / when you were twelve?
_____

8 what / do / after school when you were young?
_____

B In pairs, ask and answer the questions in exercise 8A.
Say what you do now that is different.

A *Which TV shows did you use to watch when you were eight?*
B *We never used to watch TV during the week, but we watched all the cartoons on Saturday morning.*
A *Do you still watch TV on Saturday morning?*
B *No, I usually meet friends. I watch TV in the evening after work.*

Write about differences between your life now and your parents' lives when they were your age with *usually* and *used to*.

2D It happened to me

1 Read the blog post quickly. Which word is missing from the title: *surprising*, *frustrating*, or *terrifying*?

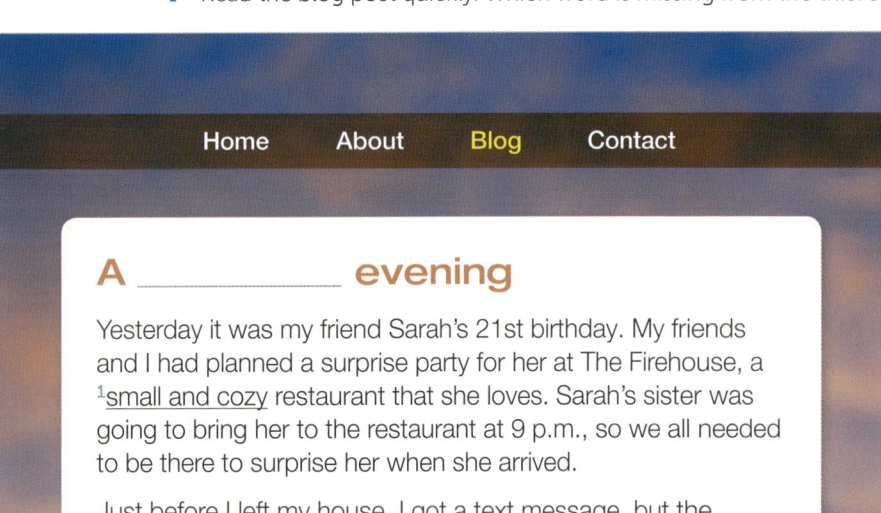

| Home | About | Blog | Contact |

A _____ evening

Yesterday it was my friend Sarah's 21st birthday. My friends and I had planned a surprise party for her at The Firehouse, a [1]small and cozy restaurant that she loves. Sarah's sister was going to bring her to the restaurant at 9 p.m., so we all needed to be there to surprise her when she arrived.

Just before I left my house, I got a text message, but the battery on my phone ran out before I could read it. I didn't have time to charge my phone, so I got in the car and left. [2]It was a horrible, rainy evening, but there wasn't much traffic, and everything was going fine until my car stopped suddenly. I'd run out of gas! [3]I was so angry with myself – [4]why hadn't I gotten some the night before?

I thought my best option would be to find a cab. After waiting for ten minutes, I finally found one. [5]I felt so relieved – I could still get to the restaurant in time. However, on the way, I realized that I'd left my wallet in my car and didn't have any money to pay! I explained this to the driver, [6]a rude and impatient man. He stopped the car and told me to get out.

[7]What a disaster! It was now almost 9 p.m., so I had to run. When I finally got to the restaurant, I was surprised to see that it was completely empty. I waited for an hour, but nobody came. So I walked back to the car, got my wallet, and took a bus home. As soon as I got home, I started charging my phone in the kitchen, but before I could call anyone, I got a message. It said, "Sarah sick, party canceled!" I didn't know whether to laugh or cry.

a ☐

b ☐

c ☐

f ☐

e ☐

d ☐

2 A Read the blog post again. Put the pictures in the correct order from 1–6.

B Cover the blog. Look at the pictures and retell the story in pairs.

> ### 🔧 Skill — making a narrative interesting
>
> **When writing a narrative, make the story more interesting by:**
> - describing people, places, and the events
> - describing emotions and feelings
> - including one or two comments about the events.

3 Read the Skill box. Match the <u>underlined</u> phrases (1–7) in the blog post with the three features of a narrative (a–c).

a descriptions of people, places, and events: _____ _____ _____

b descriptions of emotions and feelings: _____ _____

c comments about the events: _____ _____

4 A Choose the correct words to complete the sentences.

> comfortable   surprised   nightmare   luckily   tall   disappointed

1 I thought Sue was on vacation, so I was _____ to see her at work.
2 _____, I had another pair of glasses in my bag.
3 She was _____, blonde, and wearing a beautiful green dress.
4 When they told me I'd failed the exam, I felt really _____.
5 The hotel room was small, but it was very _____.
6 The train had already left, and I had lost my ticket. What a _____!

B Which of the features a–c in exercise 3 does each sentence in 4A use?

> ### 🧩 Text builder — time linkers
>
> We use time linkers like *before*, *after*, *until*, and *as soon as* to make the order of two past actions clear:
> *Just **before** I left my house, I got a text message.*   *Everything was going fine **until** my car stopped suddenly.*
> ***After** waiting for ten minutes, I finally got a cab.*   ***As soon as** I got home, I started charging my phone.*
>
> **Look!** After *before* and *after*, we can use a verb + *-ing* or a subject and verb. After *until* and *as soon as*, we can only use a subject and verb:
> *As soon as I arrived, I went to bed.* NOT *As soon as arriving, I went to bed.*

5 A Read the Text builder. In each of the four example sentences, which action happened first? Discuss in pairs.

B Complete the sentences with the correct time linker.

1 It was raining, so I waited in my car *until / as soon as* my sister's train arrived.
2 *Before / After* she got off the train, she checked that she had all of her things.
3 They sent their parents a text *until / as soon as* their plane landed in Buenos Aires.
4 *After / Until* he closed the door, he realized that he had left his keys inside the apartment.
5 *Before / As soon as* I got home, I started to cook dinner.
6 *As soon as / After* driving him home, she went to get some gas.

6 A **PREPARE** Think about something amazing, surprising, frustrating, or terrifying that happened to you. Make notes about the main events and any descriptions or comments you want to include to make your story more interesting.

B **PRACTICE** Write a blog post, using your notes to help you. Include different narrative tenses and time linkers.

C **PERSONAL BEST** Exchange your blog post with your partner. Read his/her work and correct any mistakes. How could you improve it? What do you like best about his/her story?

Personal Best Read the blog post on page 18 again. Close your book and write a one-paragraph summary of it.

Grammar

1 Choose the correct options to complete the sentences.

1 I usually _____ my e-mails in the morning.
   a am checking   **b** check   **c** was checking

2 What _____ last weekend?
   a did you   **b** do you do   **c** did you do

3 While I _____ for my cab, my girlfriend called.
   a waited   **b** had waited   **c** was waiting

4 When I lived in London, I _____ ride my bike to work.
   a usually   **b** used to   **c** use to

5 Sorry, I can't talk now. We _____ dinner.
   a 're having   **b** had   **c** have

6 Who _____ that bar of chocolate?
   a did you give   **b** gave you   **c** did give you

7 I couldn't go to the concert because they _____ all the tickets the day before.
   a were selling   **b** sold   **c** had sold

8 Where _____ to go on vacation when you were young?
   a did you used   **b** did you use   **c** you used

2 Rewrite the sentences using the tenses or phrases in parentheses.

1 Sam plays tennis in the park with his brother. (present continuous)
   Sam _____ tennis in the park with his brother.

2 The ground is very wet because it rained all night. (simple past, past perfect)
   The ground _____ very wet because it _____ all night.

3 What do you do with your friends on the weekend? (simple past)
   What _____ with your friends on the weekend?

4 Jack was out of shape when he was in school. (*used to*)
   Jack _____ out of shape when he was in school.

5 He's using his tablet to check Facebook. (simple present)
   He _____ his tablet to check Facebook.

6 At nine o'clock last night, I took a bath. (past continuous)
   At nine o'clock last night, I _____ a bath.

7 Who does she live with? (simple past)
   Who _____ with?

8 Who takes the children to school every day? (*used to*)
   Who _____ the children to school?

3 Choose the correct options to complete the text.

Saved by a kitten

Yuriko Morota is a professional musician from Tokyo in Japan. She [1]*plays / is playing* the piano for a living. Last week, Yuriko [2]*had shared / shared* an amazing story about her uncle on her Twitter account. Apparently, her uncle lived in Tokyo and [3]*used to have / usually has* a beautiful cat called Nikko. Yuriko [4]*doesn't like / isn't liking* cats, but she loved Nikko because he [5]*was saving / had saved* her uncle's life. One day, her uncle [6]*went / was going* to the airport to catch a plane when he [7]*was seeing / saw* an abandoned kitten on the street – its owners [8]*were leaving / had left* it outside. Yuriko's uncle [9]*was loving / loved* cats, so he [10]*took / had taken* the kitten home with him. Because of this, he [11]*missed / was missing* his flight. The following morning he [12]*listened / was listening* to the radio when he [13]*was hearing / heard* that his plane [14]*crashed / had crashed* into the mountains 100 km. from Tokyo. He couldn't believe how lucky he was!

Vocabulary

1 Circle the word or phrase that is different. Explain your answer.

1 check your e-mails   get a text message
   speak face-to-face   give someone a call

2 a story   congratulations
   a joke   the truth

3 go out   bring up
   break up   pay back

4 excited   terrified
   depressed   embarrassed

5 a lie   slowly
   a language   loudly

6 fascinating   amazing
   annoying   exciting

2 Match the words in the box with definitions 1–8.

> keep in touch with   go up   amusing   try on
> bring up   go back   fascinating   run out of

1 something that makes you smile or laugh _____
2 care for a child until he/she is an adult _____
3 return _____
4 communicate regularly with _____
5 have no more of _____
6 very interesting _____
7 put on clothes before buying them to see if they fit _____
8 increase _____

3 Choose the correct options to complete the sentences.

1 I _____ a lot of my photos on social media.
   a give   b share   c send
2 It was very _____ because I couldn't remember her name.
   a exciting   b disappointing c embarrassing
3 We ended _____ having dinner at home last night.
   a again   b up   c back
4 My grandpa _____ us a really funny joke last night.
   a told   b said   c talked
5 I think it's polite to _____ to e-mails on the same day.
   a answer   b check   c reply
6 My mother was really _____ because the cab was twenty minutes late.
   a amazed   b amused   c annoyed
7 I didn't know you could _____ Japanese!
   a talk   b speak   c say
8 Hurry _____ ! I don't want to be late for work.
   a off   b on   c up

4 Complete the e-mail with the words in the box.

> shocking   said   face   told   out   talk   spoke
> depressed   checked   gotten   broken   call

Hi Anna,
When I ¹_____ my phone this morning I saw that I'd ²_____ a text message from Chloe. So I decided to give her a ³_____ . When I ⁴_____ to her she seemed pretty ⁵_____ . She ⁶_____ me that her boyfriend had ⁷_____ up with her, and she wanted to ⁸_____ to someone about it. They've been going ⁹_____ together for three years, so it was very ¹⁰_____ when he ¹¹_____ he'd met someone else. Anyway, we're going to get together for coffee later, as it's always better to speak to someone ¹²_____-to-face.
Hope to see you soon!
Love,
Sophie

Personal **Best**

Lesson 1A
Describe three things you did yesterday using communication phrases.

Lesson 2A
Name five -ed adjectives that describe your feelings today.

Lesson 1A
Describe three things that you are/aren't doing now.

Lesson 2A
Write a sentence using the simple past and past continuous.

Lesson 1B
Write one sentence with *actually* and one with *in fact*.

Lesson 2A
Write a sentence using the simple past and past perfect.

Lesson 1C
Name five phrases with *say* and *tell*.

Lesson 2B
Write two sentences about a friend using phrasal verbs.

Lesson 1C
Write two object questions and two subject questions.

Lesson 2C
Name something you used to do and something you didn't use to do when you were a teenager.

Lesson 1D
Write three questions you can use to make small talk.

Lesson 2D
Write four sentences about the past using these time linkers: *before, after, until,* and *as soon as.*

People

3A It's a plan

1 Look at the words in the box. Which adjectives describe your personality?

> kind   sociable   patient   generous   hardworking   organized   responsible

Personal Best

Go to Vocabulary practice: personality adjectives, page 139

2 In pairs, think of three adjectives to describe:

a a good boss   b a good teacher   c a good friend

3 A Read the text. <u>Underline</u> the personality adjectives.

Planning
personalities

You can tell a lot about people by the way they organize their social life. Here are four types of planners we probably all know.

The last-minute planner is very easygoing, calls you ten minutes before an event, and is surprised when you can't come!

The **disorganized** planner never uses a calendar and often plans to do two things at the same time, sometimes forgetting both!

The **plan-ahead** planner is extremely organized and likes to make detailed plans a long time before the event, expecting everyone else to do the same.

The **unreliable** planner makes plans, but cancels just before you're going to meet and doesn't think this is a problem.

B Read the text again. Ask and answer the questions in pairs.

1 Do you have any friends who make plans like this?   **2** What kind of planner are you?

4 A ▶ **3.3** Listen to four voicemail messages. Which type of planner is each person?

Ben _____   Zoe _____   Eva _____   Jack _____

B ▶ **3.3** Who said the sentences: Ben (B), Zoe (Z), Eva (E), or Jack (J)? Listen again and check.

1 I'm going to cook Japanese food for you.   _____
2 I'm going to stay at home and watch TV.   _____
3 How about coffee at 4 p.m. instead? I won't forget, I promise.   _____
4 I have my sister's car – I'll come and get you if you'd like.   _____
5 My friend's band is playing at 9:30.   _____
6 I'm having lunch with my brother tomorrow.   _____

5 **A** Match the forms with the sentences in exercise 4B.

present continuous _____ _____   future with *be going to* _____ _____   future with *will* _____ _____

B Match the sentences in 4B with the correct functions (a–c). Then read the Grammar box.

a a plan or intention _____ _____   **c** a promise   _____

b an offer   _____

📖 **Grammar** **future forms: present continuous, *be going to*, and *will***

Future plans and intentions:

We're meeting at the restaurant at eight thirty   He's going to learn another language.

Promises, offers, and instant decisions:

I'll help you with your homework tomorrow.   I'll carry your bags for you.   I'll text her.

Go to Grammar practice: future forms: present continuous, *be going to*, and *will*, page 116

6 **A** ▶ 3.5 **Pronunciation:** *going to* Listen to the conversation. When is *going to* pronounced "gonna"?

A Are you going to the beach this weekend?
B No, I think I'm going to visit my parents. And you?
A I'm going to take the bus to the beach on Friday night. I can't wait.
B You're so lucky! I'm going to the beach the weekend after.

B In pairs, practice the conversation. Use the two different pronunciations of *going to*.

7 **A** Match text messages 1–5 with responses a–e.

1 I'_____ (go) away this weekend, but I can't take my dog with me. ☹

2 Help! My tablet has a virus!

3 You ate all my chocolate! ☹

4 I can't believe how terrible the band was last night.

5 I hear you'_____ _____ (get) married next year. Congratulations! ☺

a I'_____ _____ (come) over right away.

b Thanks! The wedding _____ _____ _____ _____ (be) in the spring, but we don't have a date yet.

c Sorry! I _____ _____ (not do) it again …

d I'_____ _____ (look) after him!

e I know. I'm never _____ _____ _____ (go) to see them again!

B Complete the text messages with the future forms of the verbs in parentheses.

Go to Communication practice: Students A and B page 158

8 In pairs, ask and answer the questions. Use future forms. Give as much information as possible and ask follow-up questions.

New Year's resolutions:
-go to the gym
-work harder
-eat less chocolate

What are your New Year's resolutions for next year?

What are you doing this weekend?

What are you going to do this summer?

What decisions have you made about your future studies or career?

Which future plans are you most excited about?

Which future plans are you not excited about?

Personal Best   Imagine you are helping to plan a party. Think of six offers you could make to help.

3B Born to rebel

1 Read the title, introduction, and headings of the text on page 25. In pairs, answer the questions.

  1 What are the four different birth orders? Which are you?

  2 According to the introduction, which child is typically a rebel? Do you agree?

2 Read the text quickly. Which people agree that their personality is typical of their birth order? Discuss your answers in pairs.

> 🔧 **Skill**   **reading for specific information**
>
> **When we want to find specific information in a text, we need to know where to look.**
> - Read the question carefully and underline key words.
> - Scan the text, looking for any synonyms or paraphrases of the underlined key words.
> - Read that part in detail.

3 Read the Skill box. Scan the text and find the information you need to match sentences 1–8 with the people.

Which person ...

  1 thinks the experience with her brothers helps with her job now?   _____

  2 works hard and doesn't like making mistakes?   _____

  3 is certain of his ability to do well and is good at making decisions?   _____

  4 used to take care of younger family members, but worried about it?   _____

  5 is good at making people agree with her, but can think about herself too much?   _____

  6 didn't like people making decisions for her and became a rebel?   _____

  7 thinks his parents' behavior made him calm, but bad at planning?   _____

  8 is happy that her brothers and sisters received more attention than her?   _____

4 **A** Look at the two sentences. <u>Underline</u> the part of each sentence that gives a reason for something. Ⓒircle the part that gives a result of something.

  1 Psychologists say that middle children become independent since they get less parental attention.

  2 Psychologists say that middle children get less parental attention, so they become independent.

  B Which two words in the sentences above express reason and result?

> 🧩 **Text builder**   **linkers of reason and result**
>
> **Reasons (*as* and *since*):**
> *I'm tired **as I slept badly**.*   *I took a cab **since it was late**.*
> **Results (*That's why* and *so*):**
> *I slept badly. **That's why I'm tired**.*   *It was late, **so I took a cab**.*

5 Read the Text builder. Rewrite the sentences from the text with the words in parentheses.

  1 I wanted to be my own person, so when I was a child I was pretty rebellious. (as)

  2 Parents usually pay more attention to their first child. That's why oldest children like me are normally confident. (since)

  3 Oldest children are often more responsible and reliable since they look after their younger siblings. (That's why)

  4 We tend to be hardworking and mature since we have our parents' full attention and support. (so)

6 Is your personality typical of your birth order, according to the text? How about your family and friends? Discuss in pairs.

The birth order effect

Many psychologists agree that your birth order influences your personality more than other factors such as your gender or culture. One belief is that oldest children identify with parents and authority, whereas youngest children often rebel against them. There are many other personality types thought to be typical of youngest, middle, oldest, and only children. But are they true? We interviewed eight people to find out.

Oldest children

Apparently, parents usually pay more attention to their first child. That's why oldest children like me are normally confident and decisive. I suppose that was true of my parents, and it made me a pretty confident person. I'm definitely not indecisive. Am I a rebel? No, not at all, I work for the police department! *Jack*

I had to help my mother with my two younger sisters. Psychologists believe that oldest children are often more responsible and reliable since they look after their younger siblings, but this can also make us pretty anxious. I'd say that's true for me, and because I've always respected my parents' authority, I accepted the responsibility and the anxiety. *Mick*

Youngest children

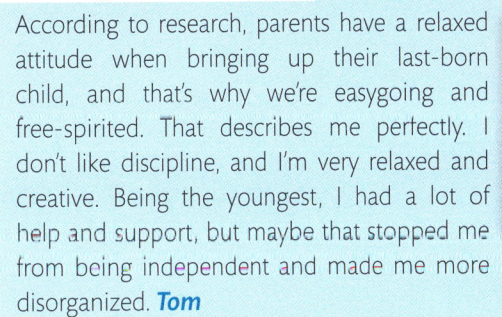

According to research, parents have a relaxed attitude when bringing up their last-born child, and that's why we're easygoing and free-spirited. That describes me perfectly. I don't like discipline, and I'm very relaxed and creative. Being the youngest, I had a lot of help and support, but maybe that stopped me from being independent and made me more disorganized. *Tom*

I grew up with older brothers and sisters who were bigger and smarter than me. They were extremely bossy – always telling me what to do, which I hated. I wanted to be my own person, so when I was a child I was pretty rebellious, which psychologists think is normal for youngest children. *Tina*

Middle children

My older sister was serious and used to prefer spending time with our parents, and my younger brother always used to get their love and attention. Because of this, I used to spend most of my time alone or with friends. Psychologists say that middle children become independent since they get less parental attention. That's definitely true in my case, and in my opinion, it was good for me. *Sara*

Research has suggested that middle children are often very competitive, but I'm the opposite – I was always trying to keep the peace between my older and younger brothers! I definitely think that's why I have good communication skills now, which helps with my career in Human Resources. *Alice*

Only children

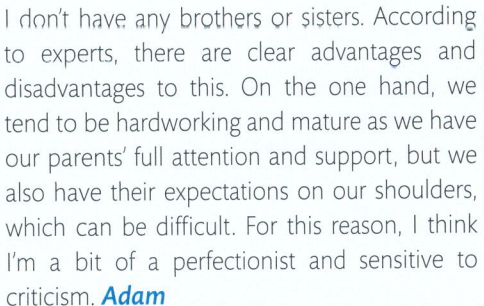

I don't have any brothers or sisters. According to experts, there are clear advantages and disadvantages to this. On the one hand, we tend to be hardworking and mature as we have our parents' full attention and support, but we also have their expectations on our shoulders, which can be difficult. For this reason, I think I'm a bit of a perfectionist and sensitive to criticism. *Adam*

As we usually got what we wanted when we were growing up, apparently it's difficult for only children to compromise. That's why we can be a bit selfish and impatient. I think that's also why I'm good at persuading people. I remember trying to persuade my parents to give me a sister for my birthday! It didn't work. *Anita*

3C Good neighbors, bad neighbors

Personal Best

1 Work in pairs. Explain the difference between:

1 a **close friend** and a **best friend**.
2 a **neighbor** and a **next-door neighbor**.
3 a **colleague** and a **classmate**.
4 a **couple** and a **partner**.
5 a **parent** and a **relative**.

Go to Vocabulary practice: relationships, page 139

2 Think of a friend, colleague, or neighbor you know well. Ask and answer the questions in pairs.

1 How do you know this person?
2 How long did it take you to get to know each other?
3 Have you ever argued or had a falling out? Why?
4 When did you last get together?
5 What do you have in common?

3 Read the notice. Do you think events like this are a good idea? Why/Why not?

WORLD NEIGHBORS' DAY

Neighbors' Day encourages people to get together, get to know each other, and develop a real sense of community.

Over 30 million people celebrated Neighbors' Day last year, helping to create better neighborhoods all over the world.

Get involved!
Your neighborhood is having the following Neighbors' Day celebration:

What:
Street party with barbecue lunch
Where:
Maple Avenue
When:
Saturday, June 13th, 2 p.m. – 7 p.m.

4 **A** ▶3.8 Listen to three people answer the question "What makes a good neighbor?" Match the opinions with the speakers: John (J), Mary (M), or Lisa (L).

1 Good neighbors help each other. _____
2 They're not noisy. _____
3 They're kind and try not to annoy other neighbors. _____

B ▶3.8 Listen again and complete the sentences with the words you hear.

John   I had a bad experience in the _____ building [1]**where I used to live**. The biggest problem was the people [2]**that lived on the first floor**. They played _____ heavy metal music all the time, and their _____ was always loud, too.

Mary   My neighbor Tony, [3]**who works as a travel agent**, is away at the moment. I'm _____ after his apartment. Once, though, another _____ did something [4]**that made me furious**. I'd given her my keys while I was away, but she _____ with her boyfriend, and when I came home, he was asleep on my sofa!

Lisa   Most people here are very _____ and considerate. And we have some _____ rules, [5]**which most people follow**. I get annoyed with some neighbors, though, like the family [6]**whose children leave bicycles in front of my door** and throw trash on my _____ .

5 Do you agree with the speakers? What do you think makes a good or bad neighbor?

6 Look at clauses 1–6 in **bold** in exercise 4B. Which relative pronouns do we use to talk about:

1 things? _____ or _____
2 people? _____ or _____
3 places? _____
4 possessions? _____

7 **A** Look at the two sentences from exercise 4B and answer the questions.

a The biggest problem was the people **that lived on the first floor**.

b My neighbor Tony, **who works as a travel agent**, is away at the moment.

1 Which relative clause is essential and identifies who or what we are talking about? _____

2 Which relative clause gives extra information, although, without it, the sentence still makes sense? _____

B Look at clauses 1–6 in exercise 4B again. Which clauses are essential? Which give extra information? Then read the Grammar box.

> **Grammar** defining and non-defining relative clauses
>
> | Defining relative clauses (identifying who or what we are talking about): | Non-defining relative clauses (giving extra information): |
> |---|---|
> | The woman **who lives above me** is a doctor. | I saw the movie, **which was great**. |
> | That's the village **where I grew up**. | That town, **where my mother grew up**, is beautiful. |
> | Do you know the man **whose car was stolen**? | My uncle, **whose house is over there**, works as a fire fighter. |
>
> **Look!** When a relative clause gives extra information, we separate it with commas (or a comma and a period).

Personal Best

Go to Grammar practice: defining and non-defining relative clauses, page 117

8 **A** ▶ 3.10 **Pronunciation:** pausing in relative clauses We usually pause before a clause that gives extra information. Listen to the sentences. Add commas where the pauses are.

1 The family who lives on my floor is really friendly.

2 My grandmother lives in Quito which is in the north of Ecuador.

3 My brother who is a chef works at the hospital.

4 I get along well with the couple who lives in the apartment next to mine.

5 I don't see my cousins who live in Argentina.

6 It's easy to park on the street where I live.

B In pairs, change the sentences in 8A so they are true for you. Add extra details if necessary.

The couple who lives on my floor is really noisy.

Go to Communication practice: Student A page 158, Student B page 168

9 **A** Choose two places, two objects, and two people that are very important to you.

Places	Objects	People
1 _____	1 _____	1 _____
2 _____	2 _____	2 _____

B In pairs, talk about your choices. Ask your partner why each of his/her choices is important, and ask for more information. Use relative clauses in your answers.

A *Tell me about one of your places.*

B *It's Montevideo.*

A *Why is it so important to you?*

B *Because it's the place where I met my boyfriend.*

A *How did you meet him?*

B *We were both in college there.*

Personal Best Write five sentences about your relatives and close friends with non-defining relative clauses.

Learning Curve

3D I have some news

1 A Look at the sentences. Which are good news? Which are bad news? Which news do you think the man in the photo has?

1 I'm afraid you didn't get the job.
2 We won the game! We're in the final!
3 I've had a falling out with my best friend.
4 Your rent's going up by 20%.
5 She said "Yes"!
6 I got a promotion.

B In pairs, discuss the questions.

1 What good news can you remember receiving in your life? What did you say?
2 Have you ever had to give someone bad news? How did you feel?

2 ▶ **3.11** Watch or listen to the first part of *Learning Curve*. Answer the questions.

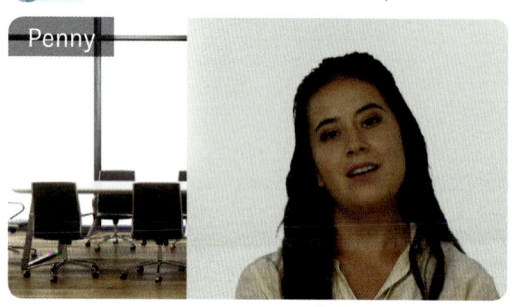
Penny

Simon

1 What news does Penny give Simon?
2 How do they both feel about the news?

3 ▶ **3.12** How did Penny give Simon the news? How did Simon respond? Listen and complete the sentences.

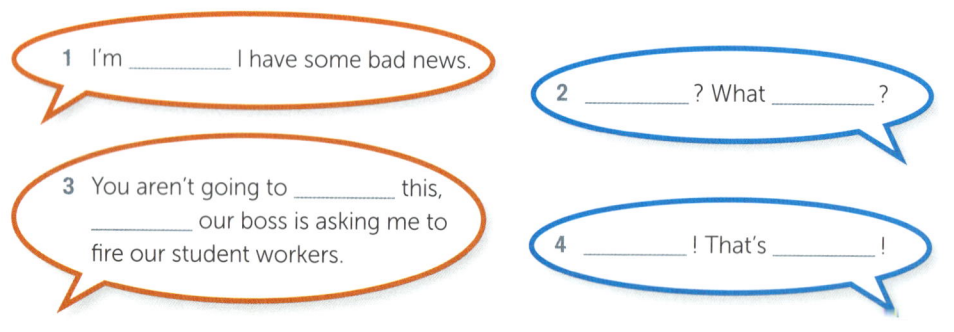

1 I'm _____ I have some bad news.

2 _____? What _____?

3 You aren't going to _____ this, _____ our boss is asking me to fire our student workers.

4 _____! That's _____!

◀▮▶ Conversation builder | giving and responding to news

Giving news	Responding to news
I'm afraid I have some bad news.	That's a relief.
I'm really sorry to say this, but ...	Oh no, that's terrible!
You aren't going to believe this, but ...	What a shame! That's too bad!
Great news! I'm ...	I'm so happy for you! That's fantastic news!
Guess what? I'm ...	I'm absolutely thrilled for you! Congratulations!

4 Read the Conversation builder. Put the phrases in the correct column in the chart.

giving good news	giving bad news	responding to good news	responding to bad news

5 **A** In pairs, complete the conversation with the words in the box.

> awful   thrilled   afraid   shame   that's   wonderful   congratulations

A Great news! I've been offered a job writing for a new magazine!
B Wow! [1]_____ fantastic news! I'm absolutely [2]_____ for you! When do you start?
A Next month. I can't wait. It's a really exciting place to work.
B That's [3]_____ ! [4]_____ !
A How are things with you?
B Well, I'm [5]_____ I have some bad news. I broke my leg last week.
A Oh no, that's [6]_____ ! What a [7]_____ ! I'm so sorry.

B In pairs, practice the conversation. You can change the details.

6 ▶ **3.13** Watch or listen to the second part of the show. Answer the questions.

1 What news does Sherry give Penny?
2 How does Penny feel about it?
3 How does Simon feel about it?

7 ▶ **3.13** How did Sherry give Penny her news? Order phrases a–h. Watch or listen again and check.

a ☐ It's in my neighborhood, much closer to my apartment.
b ☐ but it's sort of bad news for you.
c ☐ It's a great opportunity to work with customers.
d ☐ Well, you know that I study fashion at college, right?
e ☐ So, I'm really sorry to say this, but I'm resigning.
f ☐ Well, it's good news for me,
g [1] I have some news.
h ☐ Well, I got a great job offer to work at a department store that I just love.

🔧 **Skill** **giving bad news**

When we give someone bad news, we often try to do it in a sensitive way.
• Prepare the person first – tell him/her you have some bad news.
• Briefly explain the situation behind the bad news.
• Say exactly what the bad news is.
• Be sympathetic – say that you're really sorry.

8 Read the Skill box. What did Sherry do to give Penny the news in a sensitive way?

Go to Communication practice: Student A page 158, Student B page 168

9 **A** **PREPARE** In pairs, look at the situations below. Think about what you will say.

	situation 1	situation 2
Student A	You've been offered an amazing job in another city, but you're worried your parents will be upset that you're leaving. Tell your mother/father the news.	You're Student B's roommate and close friend. Listen and respond to the news. Ask questions and continue the conversation.
Student B	You're Student A's mother/father. Listen and respond to the news. Ask questions and continue the conversation.	Your cousin has just moved into a fantastic apartment and wants you to rent the spare room. You're worried your current roommate will be upset that you're leaving. Tell him/her the news.

B **PRACTICE** In pairs, take turns giving your news and responding to it.

C **PERSONAL BEST** How could you improve the way you gave the news and responded to your partner's news? Find another partner and give your news again.

Places and homes

4A What makes your city great?

1 What three things make your town or city great? Discuss your answers in pairs.

2 Look at the text about four cities below. According to each writer, what makes his/her city great?

I ♥ MY CITY

With Melbourne topping the list of the best cities in the world to live, we celebrate cities everywhere, and invite you to share what you love about your city. #whatmakesyourcitygreat

David

What I love most about this city are the parks and green spaces. When you have a little free time, there's always an open space, urban park, or secret garden nearby where you can go to relax. One really interesting project, the High Line, is a 2.3 km. long park built on an elevated section of a former railway line. It's a wonderful pedestrian area and has fabulous views of the Hudson River, Manhattan, and the New York City skyline.

Kiyomi

The nightlife here is amazing. There are plenty of places to go and things to do in the evening, with thousands of cafés, restaurants, and nightclubs. But what I like best about Tokyo are the unusual places to eat out. Last week, I had dinner at the seafood restaurant Zauo, where the tables are on a boat and you catch your own fish from the aquarium, which the chefs then cook for you. It was lots of fun!

Klaus

In most big cities, there aren't enough roads that are safe for bicycling. But here in Copenhagen, there are over 400 km. of bike paths, so you can ride everywhere with no danger, avoiding traffic jams and staying in shape at the same time. There aren't many people who regularly use a car here – in fact, most people go to work or school by bike or on foot. Some use the Cycle Snake, an elevated bike path over the harbor. It was built especially for bicyclists, and the views from it are spectacular!

Lola

New Orleans sure has rhythm! You hear live music on almost every street: there's always a jazz band playing, or a few musicians jamming together in a café or on a street corner. My favorite time of year is Mardi Gras – the famous carnival celebration with music and colorful parades. Some people complain that there are too many tourists here at Mardi Gras, but I think everyone should be able to see the greatest free show on Earth!

3 Match the words in each box to make compound nouns. Check your answers in the text.

| bike   traffic   pedestrian   night | | area   life   jam   path |

Go to Vocabulary practice: compound nouns, page 140

4 Read the text again. Are the sentences true (T) or false (F)? Correct the false sentences.

1 There aren't many green spaces in New York. _____
2 There are trains on the High Line. _____
3 It's not dangerous to ride a bike in Copenhagen. _____
4 Cars aren't allowed on the Cycle Snake. _____
5 In Tokyo, the restaurants are all pretty similar. _____
6 At Zauo, customers catch the fish and cook it. _____
7 There's live music everywhere in New Orleans. _____
8 A lot of tourists visit New Orleans for Mardi Gras. _____

5 Which city sounds like the best one to live in? Why? Discuss your answers in pairs.

6 Look at the highlighted words in the text. Put them in the correct category. Then read the Grammar box.

1 small quantities: not much, _____ , _____ , _____

2 large quantities: a lot of, _____ , _____

3 zero quantity: not any, _____

4 more or less than necessary: too much, _____ , _____

Grammar quantifiers

Small quantities:

There's **not**/There **isn't much** time, hurry up!
There **aren't many** people on this beach.
Can I have **a little** cake and **a few** cookies, please?

Zero quantity:

There's **no** bread/There **isn't any** bread.

Large quantities:

We have **a lot of/lots of** work today.
There are **plenty of** bananas if you're hungry.

More or less than necessary:

There's **too much** traffic. There are **too many** cars.
There's **not**/There **isn't enough** ice cream for everyone.

Go to Grammar practice: quantifiers, page 118

7 A ▶ 4.3 **Pronunciation:** sentence stress Listen to the sentences. Which syllables are stressed?

1 I've been to a lot of museums.

2 I don't go to many concerts.

3 I know a few nice restaurants.

4 There are plenty of stores in my area.

5 My friends don't have enough free time.

6 There's no live music in my town.

7 It's too noisy where I live.

8 There's too much stress in my life.

B ▶ 4.3 Listen again and repeat the sentences.

8 Change the sentences in exercise 7A so they are true for you. Compare your sentences in pairs.

9 ▶ 4.4 Choose the correct quantifiers to complete the text. Listen and check.

not enough   a few   a little   plenty of   too   too many

Melbourne number 1, again!

Melbourne has come first again in the list of the best places to live. Only [1]_____ cities like Zurich and Vancouver have come first more than once, but Melbourne has won it for the fifth consecutive year! It's such an interesting and vibrant city, with [2]_____ things to do. The climate is great – it's never [3]_____ hot or cold, which makes it perfect for strolling around the harbor or the pedestrian areas downtown and admiring the colorful street art. If you like [4]_____ culture, spend a day exploring the city's museums, art galleries, and the Arts Centre, which looks like the Eiffel Tower! Getting around is easy, too, but with more than a million people driving into the city every day, there are [5]_____ traffic jams and [6]_____ parking spaces. Taking the streetcar is easy and convenient, though.

Go to Communication practice: Student A page 159, Student B page 168

10 Discuss what you think of the following things in your city in pairs.

downtown   public transportation   pedestrian areas   nightlife   art galleries   parking lots

bike paths   department stores   shopping malls   nightclubs   traffic jams   sports centers

A *In my opinion, there aren't enough pedestrian areas here.*

B *You're right. There's too much traffic, so we need more pedestrian areas.*

Personal Best   Write five sentences about what an ideal city would be like. Use a quantifier in each sentence.

31

4B City or country?

1 In pairs, make a list of advantages and disadvantages of living in the city and living in the country.

2 Complete the sentences with the verbs in the box. Which sentences are about living in the city? Which sentences are about living in the country?

> have (x2)   catch   meet (x2)   miss (x2)   take

1 It's easy to _____ a friend and _____ coffee or a snack.
2 It's difficult to _____ new people.
3 I _____ the peace and quiet and being surrounded by nature.
4 Public transportation isn't great. If you _____ a bus, you have to wait ages to _____ the next one, or ask someone to _____ you by car.
5 The nightlife's great. It's easy to go out and _____ a good time.

3 Which sentences in exercise 2 are true for where you live?

Go to Vocabulary practice: common verb phrases, page 141

🔧 **Skill** **understanding key points**

When people speak, listen for the key points of the ideas they talk about.
- People often emphasize the key points and can use expressions such as *most importantly*, *the main thing is*.
- They often repeat the key points using different words.
- They often give examples, reasons, and more information to support the key points.

4 A ▶ **4.6** Read the Skill box. Watch or listen to the first part of *Learning Curve*. Kate talks about studies on city and country life. Check (✔) the three key points.

1 People who live in the country live longer. ☐
2 People who live in the city are more stressed out. ☐
3 Country life is better when you work in the city. ☐
4 Young adults prefer to live in the city. ☐
5 Retired people prefer to live in the country. ☐

Kate

B ▶ **4.6** Compare your answers in pairs. Watch or listen again and check.

5 ▶ **4.7** Watch or listen to the second part of the show. Where do Tracy, Carlos, and Sing live and work? Check (✔) the correct options in the chart.

Tracy

Carlos

Sing

	lives in the ...		works in the ...	
	city	country	city	country
Tracy				
Carlos				
Sing				

6 **A** ▶ **4.7** Watch or listen again. Are the sentences true or false? Correct the incorrect sentences.

1 Tracy loves where she lives because it's quiet. _____
2 She likes knowing all her neighbors. _____
3 She doesn't like commuting to work. _____
4 Carlos thinks city life is very convenient. _____
5 He misses the country. _____
6 He enjoys having a lot of options for going out. _____
7 Sing's a chef. _____
8 He grows vegetables on the roof of a large building. _____

B Who do you think has the best quality of life, Tracy, Carlos, or Sing?

🧩➔ **Listening builder** linking similar consonant sounds

When a word ends in a consonant sound and the next word starts with the same consonant sound, we only pronounce the sound once, not twice. The linked sounds are not always the same letter.

It's similar.   *Ethan knows.*   *We go to a sports center.*

7 ▶ **4.8** Read the Listening builder. Look at the sentences and mark where the consonant links are. Listen and check. Then practice saying the sentences.

1 It's an old house, so it took three years to modernize it.
2 It's easy to keep in touch with them.
3 We get together every weekend.
4 I just took a photo of it.
5 See you next time.

8 **A** Discuss these questions with a partner.

1 Would you prefer to live and work in the city or the country? Why?
2 How far would you be happy to travel to work or school every day? Why?
3 Where would you prefer to spend a weekend away, in a city or in the country? Why?

B Change partners. Discuss the key points of your conversation in 8A with your new partner.

Personal Best Imagine you've moved to the country. Write a paragraph about what you like about country life and what you miss about the city. **33**

4C A place to stay in NYC

1 **A** What kinds of accommodations is the website advertising? What are the advantages and disadvantages of using a website like this?

B Look at three places to stay in New York. Which one do you prefer? Why?

● reservedirect.com – find your perfect vacation home

Reserve directly with homeowners and hosts around the world. Stay in someone's home and really experience local life.

Studio apartment near Central Park

Modern, stylish studio apartment, 30 sq. m, with double bed, bathroom, and kitchen. TV, WiFi, and air conditioning.
Good location: a short distance from the Museum of Modern Art and Times Square. $175 per night

Houseboat for rent

Cozy houseboat with sofa bed. Kitchen with fridge and microwave. Shower room. Amazing views of the Empire State Building and Manhattan skyscrapers.
Location: New Jersey; short walk to Manhattan ferry. $95 per night

Artist's house in Harlem

Two comfortable, bright and spacious double rooms in our beautiful Victorian house. Full breakfast provided. Eat with other guests and your friendly hosts. Fashionable neighborhood. Close to subway station. $140 per night

2 Match the definitions with the highlighted words in the text.

1 very light _____   3 not old _____   5 big _____
2 fashionable _____   4 warm and comfortable _____

Personal Best

Go to Vocabulary practice: describing homes, page 142

3 How would you describe your home on *reservedirect.com*? Tell your partner what kind of home it is, where it is, and what it's like.

4 **A** ▶ 4.12 Listen to Jon and Louise deciding where to stay in New York. Choose the correct advantage and disadvantage they mention for each place.

accommodation	advantages	disadvantages
studio apartment	[1]*modern / convenient*	[2]*too expensive / too small*
houseboat	[3]*cheap / cozy*	[4]*uncomfortable bed / basic*
artist's house	[5]*fashionable area / convenient*	[6]*expensive / shared bathroom*

B Which place do they choose?

5 **A** ▶ 4.13 In pairs, complete the sentences from the conversation with the adjectives in the box. Listen and check.

expensive   big   fashionable   convenient   comfortable   cheaper

1 It's *by far* the most _____ .
2 Well, it's as _____ as our old apartment.
3 It's *far* _____ than the other two places.
4 We don't need to stay in one of the most _____ areas in New York.
5 A sofa bed isn't as _____ as a normal bed, is it?
6 It's *slightly* less _____ than the studio apartment.

B Look at the sentences in 5A and answer the questions. Then read the Grammar box.

1 Which sentences are comparatives? Which are superlatives?
2 Which comparative form means that two things are the same?
3 Which word and phrase in *italics* mean "a lot"? Which word means "a little"?

📖 **Grammar** **comparatives and superlatives, *as ... as***

Comparatives (two things):
*That apartment is **slightly bigger than** ours.*
*Our new sofa is **far more comfortable**.*
*Jack's apartment is **less spacious than** our house.*
*Your kitchen is **as big as** Robert's.*

Look! We can use ***slightly*** for a small difference and ***far*** for a big difference.

Superlatives (three or more things):
*This is **the nicest** present I've **ever** received.*
*It's one of **the most expensive** cities **in the world**.*
*This is **by far the least fashionable** part of town.*

Look! We can use ***by far*** to emphasize a superlative.

Go to Grammar practice: comparatives and superlatives, *as ... as*, page 119

6 A ▶ 4.15 **Pronunciation:** /ə/ sound Listen to the sentences. Notice the /ə/ sound in the underlined parts of the words.

1 It's cheap<u>er</u> th<u>an</u> my old house.
2 Apartments aren't <u>as</u> expensive <u>as</u> houses.

3 It's th<u>e</u> biggest apartment I've ev<u>er</u> seen!
4 Is there a nic<u>er</u> hotel th<u>an</u> this one?

B ▶ 4.15 Listen again and repeat the sentences.

7 Complete the sentences with the correct form of the adjectives in parentheses, and any other words needed.

1 Sit on the sofa! It's much _____ the floor. (comfortable)
2 The team that wins the World Cup is _____ team _____ the world. (good)
3 I'm going to be late! This is by far _____ bus I've _____ taken! (slow)
4 It's 75 sq. m. – It's slightly _____ my apartment, which is 70 sq. m. (spacious)
5 Villages aren't _____ towns. (big)
6 The song "Happy" is one of Pharrell Williams' _____ songs. (famous)

8 Complete the sentences with comparatives. Use the adjectives in the box or your own ideas. Compare your sentences in pairs.

enjoyable exciting boring cheap expensive
relaxing stressful difficult easy comfortable
convenient tasty spicy

Italian food isn't as tasty as Mexican food.

1 Italian food _____ Mexican food.
2 English _____ Chinese.
3 Soccer _____ tennis.
4 Being a teacher _____ being a student.
5 Being married _____ being single.
6 Living in a small town _____ living in a city.

Go to Communication practice: Student A page 159, Student B page 169

9 In pairs, ask and answer questions with the words in the chart.

Who	is/are	the best	meal	in the world?	
What	was/were	the most beautiful	city		been on?
Which		the funniest	movie		met?
		the most exciting	shoes		visited?
		the tastiest	person		eaten?
		the most stressful	country	you've ever	had?
		the most expensive	vacation		read?
		the scariest	day		bought?
		the most interesting	book		seen?
			team		known?

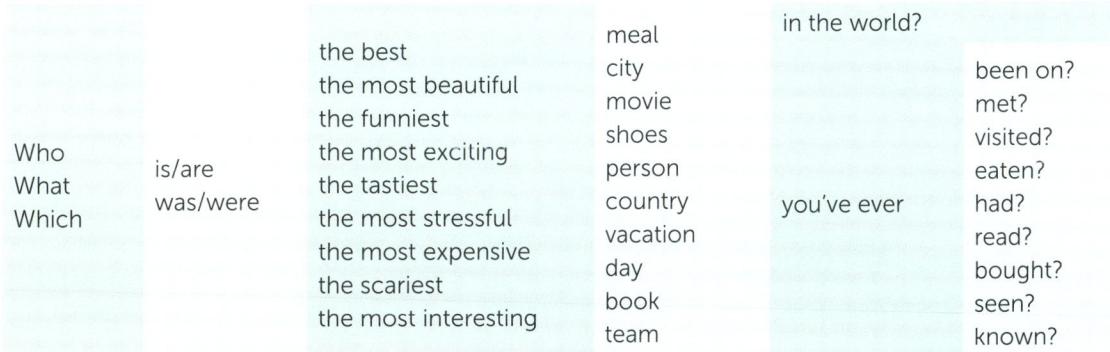

Personal Best Choose two famous people and write four sentences to compare them.

4D Hope to hear from you soon!

1 Look at the picture. What is happening? Read the e-mail and check.

● ● ●

Subject: **News**

Hey Pete,

1 Great to hear from you! Sorry for not writing sooner, but I've been really busy.

2 That's fantastic news about your master's. You're so lucky! Raleigh is such a beautiful city, and the university's great. I'm sure you'll do really well – you've always been hardworking. Don't forget to have some fun though! So, when do classes start? Have you found a place to live yet?

3 Anyway, I have some great news, too. Did I tell you I applied for a job in San Francisco a few months ago? Well, I got the job! I'm an assistant website designer. It's much more interesting than my old marketing job, and San Francisco's an amazing place. I only got here last week, but I've already found a really cool apartment to rent (see photo). It's not as big as my old place, but it's very bright and modern. I can get downtown, where I work, in under ten minutes. Convenient!

4 Why don't you come to San Francisco for vacation this summer? I'd love to see you, and we could explore the city and enjoy the nightlife!

5 By the way, do you remember Ruth Taylor from high school? Well, she works here, too! I couldn't believe it when I saw her on my first day in the office. She's just as funny as she was when we were in high school. It's so nice to have someone at work I already know.

6 Speaking of work, I'd better get back to it because I have a report to finish by tomorrow. It's only my first week, and I'm already pretty busy here.

Hope to hear from you soon!

Lots of love,

Yasmin

2 Read the e-mail again and answer the questions.
1 What is Pete going to do in Raleigh?
2 Why has Yasmin moved to San Francisco?

3 Match paragraphs 1–6 with e-mail functions a–f.
a inviting _____ c a reason to end the e-mail _____ e responding to news _____
b giving news _____ d opening comments _____ f giving more news _____

🔧 **Skill** writing an informal e-mail

We write informal e-mails to people we know well, such as friends, family members, and colleagues.
• Use contractions like *it's* and *can't*.
• Use incomplete sentences like *Great to hear from you, Sorry for not writing sooner, Can't wait to see you!*
• Use informal greetings and endings like *Hey/Hi, How are things? Lots of love, See you soon, All the best,* and *Take care*.
• Start a new paragraph for each new topic to make your e-mail easy to read.

4 Read the Skill box. Find the informal sentences in the e-mail that have the same meaning as the more formal sentences 1–8.
1 Thank you very much for your e-mail.
2 I apologize for not replying immediately.
3 I was very pleased to hear about your program.
4 When does your school program begin?
5 I also have some very good news.
6 I was offered the position.
7 I have already found a very nice apartment.
8 I should continue working.

5 Read Pete's reply to Yasmin's e-mail. Order sentences a–g.

○ ○ ○

Subject: **News**

Hi Yas,

a ☐ Anyway, I have to go, I have a meeting with my advisor in 20 minutes. Speak soon! Don't forget to let me know about July.

b ☐ **Anyway,** I have some great news. Do you remember my British cousin, Mo?

c 1 Great to hear from you! Really happy you're enjoying your new job in San Francisco.

d ☐ **So,** have you made any new friends there yet?

e ☐ **Speaking of** invitations, I'd love to visit you in San Francisco. How about the first two weeks of July? Can't wait to see you!

f ☐ **By the way,** why don't we get together with Ruth Taylor for coffee when I come? I haven't seen her in ages.

g ☐ Well, he's getting married in Brighton in March, and he's invited me to the wedding. I'm really looking forward to it. I already have a new suit (see photo). What do you think?

Take care,

Pete

6 Pete wrote his e-mail in four paragraphs. Which lines of the e-mail (a–g) do you think he included in each paragraph?

Paragraph 1 _____   Paragraph 3 _____
Paragraph 2 _____   Paragraph 4 _____

7 Look at the words in **bold** in exercise 5. Which two have a similar meaning?

✦→ **Text builder**   **informal discourse markers**

We use informal discourse markers to link ideas and help the reader understand the organization of our ideas. We can also use these in informal spoken English.

To change the subject:
Anyway, I have some great news, too.   So, when do classes start?

To introduce a less important subject:
By the way, do you remember Ruth Taylor from high school?

To return to a subject:
It's so nice to have someone at work I already know. Speaking of work, I'd better get back to it …

8 Read the Text builder. Complete the sentences with discourse markers. Compare your answers in pairs.

1 There's a new department store near my apartment. _____ shopping, have you heard about that new online store?
2 Important news! Jamie just moved to Boston because he got a new job with the Boston Globe! _____ , he's started playing soccer.
3 I'm not really enjoying my job at the moment … _____ , how did your exam go?
4 I'm hoping to get a job soon, so I can share an apartment with some friends. _____ housing, have you moved yet?

9 **A** **PREPARE** Think of a friend or family member who recently gave you some news. Plan how to respond to the news, decide what news you'd like to give, and invite him/her to do something.

B **PRACTICE** Write your e-mail. Use the ideas in the Skill box and the Text builder to help you.

C **PERSONAL BEST** Exchange your e-mail with a partner. Read his/her e-mail. Do the paragraphs and discourse markers help you understand the organization of ideas?

Personal Best Write a reply to your partner's e-mail. Respond to his/her news and give more news of your own.

Grammar

1 Cross (**X**) the sentence that is NOT correct.

1   a   I'm taking my driving test at 3:30 this afternoon. ☐
    b   I'm going to take my driving test next year. ☐
    c   I'll take my driving test at 3:30 this afternoon. ☐

2   a   He's the man whose brother is a pop singer. ☐
    b   He's the man which went out with Jenny. ☐
    c   He's the man Jenny used to go out with. ☐

3   a   There aren't no tickets left for the concert. ☐
    b   There aren't any tickets left for the concert. ☐
    c   There are no tickets left for the concert. ☐

4   a   I think it's the funniest movie I've ever seen. ☐
    b   I think it's the most funny movie I've ever seen. ☐
    c   I think it's funnier than the last movie we saw. ☐

5   a   It's after midnight. Should I call you a cab? ☐
    b   It's after midnight. Do I call you a cab? ☐
    c   It's after midnight. I'll call you a cab. ☐

6   a   Uncle Jack, who works as an accountant, lives
        in Sydney. ☐
    b   Jack is my uncle who works as an accountant
        in Sydney. ☐
    c   Uncle Jack, that works as an accountant, lives
        in Sydney. ☐

7   a   His new apartment isn't big enough for four people. ☐
    b   His new apartment isn't enough big for four people. ☐
    c   His new apartment is too small for four people. ☐

8   a   It's one of the expensivest restaurants in my city. ☐
    b   It's one of the most expensive restaurants in my
        city. ☐
    c   It's much more expensive than the other
        restaurants in my city. ☐

2 Use the words in parentheses to complete the sentences
so they mean the same as the first sentence.

1   I plan to spend three weeks in Mexico next year.
    I _____ three weeks in Mexico next year. (going to)

2   She's the woman. She lives on the second floor.
    She's the woman _____ on the second floor. (who)

3   There were only a few people at the party.
    There _____ at the party. (many)

4   Sam is more helpful than Tom.
    Tom _____ Sam. (as ... as)

5   Would you like a cup of coffee?
    _____ make you a cup of coffee? (I)

6   That's my sister's new car. She bought it from my cousin.
    That's my sister's new car, _____ from my cousin.
    (which)

7   Nicholas is too young to drive a car.
    Nicholas _____ to drive a car. (old)

8   My brother is more generous than my sister.
    My sister is _____ my brother. (less)

3 Choose the correct options to complete the text.

The place ¹*that / where* Maria Simonetti lives is very unusual.
It is a little village in the south of Italy ²*which / who* has over
300 centenarians – people ³*which / who* are 100 years old or
more. So although Maria ⁴*is celebrating / should celebrate*
her 100th birthday next month, she's not ⁵*by far / one of* the
oldest people in her village, as over 50 of the inhabitants of
the village are over 110. Maria's seven grandchildren,
⁶*who / that* are all in their sixties, are organizing a
big party to celebrate, and ⁷*they're going to / they will*
invite her relatives and friends from all over Italy. Her
⁸*most young / youngest* grandson, Filippo, is a chef, and
⁹*he'll / he's going to* bake her a special cake with ten candles
on it, one for each decade of her life. So, what's her secret?
Well, everyone says Maria's a very sociable and positive
person. She still has a ¹⁰*few / little* friends and relatives in the
village, and someone visits her every day. Also, Maria has a
very healthy diet. She eats ¹¹*much / lots of* fish, vegetables,
and fruit, and she doesn't eat ¹²*much / many* sugar or salt.

Vocabulary

1 (Circle) the word or phrase that is different. Explain your answer.

1   modern   tiny
    comfortable   impatient

2   friendly   next-door neighbor
    close friend   classmate

3   bike path   art gallery
    shopping mall   sports center

4   easygoing   polite
    unreliable   helpful

5   confident   huge
    sensitive   kind

6   town   country
    balcony   suburbs

7   stay in shape   keep in touch
    get along   make up

8   roof terrace   pedestrian area
    basement   first floor

2 Match the words in the box with definitions 1–8.

> unsociable   traffic jam   get along well   anxious
> department store   basement   cozy   parents

1 a part of a building that is below the ground _____
2 comfortable and warm _____
3 a large store with different sections _____
4 does not enjoy being with other people _____
5 a person's mother and father _____
6 worried and afraid _____
7 have a friendly relationship _____
8 a line of cars that is not moving _____

3 Choose the correct options to complete the sentences.

1 Can you _____ me to your cousin, Sarah?
   a meet   b get to know   c introduce
2 I _____ my girlfriend at a party.
   a knew   b met   c kept
3 I enjoy working here as my _____ are friendly.
   a colleagues   b classmates   c couples
4 My team played very badly, and _____ the game 4–0.
   a won   b lost   c missed
5 I've invited all my _____ to my wedding.
   a parents   b relationships   c relatives
6 I usually _____ my friends on the weekend.
   a get together with   b get to know   c get along well with
7 He was late for work as he _____ his train.
   a caught   b lost   c missed
8 My apartment is on the top _____ .
   a balcony   b floor   c terrace

4 Complete the e-mail with the words in the box.

> basement   helpful   first floor   parking lot   spacious
> convenient   next-door neighbor   apartment building

● ● ●

Hi Adam,

I have the keys to my new place! It's on the ¹_____ of a large ²_____ . It has two bedrooms, so it's pretty ³_____ . There's a ⁴_____ in the ⁵_____ of the building where I can leave my car. It's really ⁶_____ . My ⁷_____ seems nice and really ⁸_____ – he's offered to carry my heavy boxes on moving day! Can you help, too?

Love,
Mel

Personal Best

Lesson 3A
Name five personality adjectives that describe your relatives.

Lesson 4A
Name five things in your city using compound nouns.

Lesson 3A
Write two sentences for future plans, and one for a promise.

Lesson 4A
Write four sentences about your classroom using quantifiers.

Lesson 3B
Write four sentences using these linkers: *as*, *since*, *that's why*, and *so*.

Lesson 4B
Name four verb phrases using *have*, *take*, *catch*, and *keep*.

Lesson 3C
Name five relationship verbs.

Lesson 4C
Describe an apartment or house you've visited using five adjectives for describing homes.

Lesson 3C
Write four sentences about someone you know using relative clauses: two defining and two non-defining.

Lesson 4C
Write five sentences to describe your city using comparative and superlative adjectives.

Lesson 3D
Give two expressions you can use to give news and two to respond to news.

Lesson 4D
Write four sentences to a friend using *anyway, so, by the way*, and *speaking of*.

Money and shopping

5A   Spend, spend, spend

1   In pairs, do the quiz. Is your partner a spender or a saver?

1 If I see something I really like on sale,

a   I usually buy it (whether I need it or not).

b   I ask for it for my birthday.

c   I don't buy it. My savings are for important things!

2 If I feel a bit down,

a   I go shopping – it's called "retail therapy"!

b   I go for ice cream.

c   I check my savings account – the numbers there always make me feel happy.

ARE YOU A SPENDER OR A SAVER?

Summer Sale Now On

3 If I see something in a store this weekend that I really want, but can't afford,

a   I'll buy it with my credit card.

b   I'll borrow money from a friend or relative.

c   I'll save up until I can afford it.

4 When my phone stops working,

a   I'll replace it with the latest model, probably the most expensive!

b   I'll replace it with a new model, but nothing too expensive.

c   I'll get a free one with the cheapest contract.

Personal Best

Go to Vocabulary practice: money, page 143

2   Work in pairs. Answer the questions.

1   Have you ever wasted money on something you've never used?

2   Would you prefer to be broke and happy, or wealthy and unhappy?

3   When you lend someone money, how long do you give him or her to pay you back?

4   If you need to borrow money from someone, who do you ask? Why?

5   When do you take money out and pay with cash? When do you prefer to pay with a card?

6   What would you like to spend your savings on?

3   ▶5.3   Listen to two friends, James and Sarah, doing the first two questions of the quiz. Are they spenders or savers?

4   **A**   ▶5.4   Complete the sentences from the conversation. Listen and check.

1   If I see something I like _____ _____ , I usually get it.

2   If you spend all your money, you won't be able to _____ _____ for a motorcycle.

3   As soon as I _____ _____ , I'll call you.

B   Look at the sentences in 4A. Underline the present tenses. Circle the future forms.

5   **A**   Match the sentences in exercise 4A with structures a–c and functions d–f. When do we use a present tense to talk about the future?

a   *if* + simple present, future with *will*   _____   d   a situation or routine that is generally true _____

b   *if* + simple present, simple present   _____   e   two connected future events   _____

c   future time word + simple present, future with *will* _____   f   a possible future event and its result   _____

B Look at the quiz questions again. Which of the structures and functions in 5A are they? Then read the Grammar box.

📖 **Grammar** | **zero and first conditional; future time clauses**

Zero conditional (routines or situations that are generally true):

*If it **rains**, I **take** an umbrella.*

First conditional (possible future events and their results):

*If it **doesn't rain**, I**'ll go** to the beach tomorrow.*

Look! In conditional sentences, we can use ***unless*** (*if ... not*):

Unless it rains, I'll go to the beach.

Future time clauses (two connected future events):

***As soon as** I **get** paid, I**'ll pay** you back.*   *We **won't eat until** you **get** home tonight.*

Look! In a future time clause, we use the simple present not *will*:

I'll do my homework when the movie ends. NOT ~~when the movie will end~~.

Personal Best

Go to Grammar practice: zero and first conditional; future time clauses, page 120

6 **A** ▶ 5.6 **Pronunciation:** intonation Listen to the conditional sentences. Notice the falling intonation.

1 Plants die if they don't get enough water.
2 If my husband has a cold, I usually catch it.
3 Unless Jo lends me $15, I won't be able to go.
4 I won't go shopping if the meeting finishes late.

B ▶ 5.6 Listen again and repeat the sentences with the same intonation.

7 **A** Choose the correct options to complete the text.

Save money without even trying

As soon as you ¹*start / will start* following these weekly tips from our money expert, Marta Benz, you'll save money without even trying!

Make your own coffee

²*If / Unless* I get up early, I never have time to make coffee before leaving for work, so it's tempting to buy some on the way to the office. Buying coffee every day might save time, but it doesn't save money. If you ³*make / 'll make* coffee at home next week, you ⁴*save / 'll save* at least $25. That's an annual saving of $1,250!

Pay with cash

I always ⁵*pay / will pay* by credit card when I ⁶*go / 'll go* shopping. It's much easier than finding an ATM. However, I ⁷*'ll / won't* take my card with me when I ⁸*go / will go* shopping next. Why? Because research shows that if people ⁹*pay / will pay* by credit card, they ¹⁰*don't / won't* realize how much they're spending. Paying with hard-earned cash is more "painful," so we spend less.

B In pairs, discuss which tip is the most helpful. Can you think of any other money-saving tips?

Go to Communication practice: Student A page 159, Student B page 169

8 Complete the sentences so they are true for you. Then compare your sentences in pairs.

1 If the weather's nice tomorrow, I _____ .
2 I'll probably _____ next week unless _____ .
3 I _____ next summer if I can afford it.
4 I _____ if I go shopping this weekend.
5 If I save enough money in the next six months, I _____ .
6 I usually _____ if I feel stressed out.
7 I'll keep studying English until _____ .
8 I _____ as soon as I get home tonight.

A *What will you do if the weather's nice tomorrow?*
B *If the weather's nice tomorrow, I'll probably go jogging. And you?*

Personal Best | Write six sentences with future time clauses, using words from the Vocabulary practice.

5B Black Friday

1 Look at the title of the text and the pictures on page 43. Discuss the questions in pairs.

1 Describe the pictures. What do you think is happening?
2 Have you bought any bargains recently? What were they? Where did you buy them?

2 What do you know about "Black Friday"? Choose the sentence that you think is correct. Then read the first paragraph and check.

1 Black Friday takes place just after Christmas.
2 On Black Friday, stores offer a lot of bargains.
3 It's called "Black Friday" because stores lose a lot of money on that day.

🔧 **Skill** identifying opinions

When you read a text that contains opinions, look for:
- phrases that introduce opinions: *it seems to me that, as far as I'm concerned, if you ask me.*
- adjectives that express opinions: *amazing, disappointing, successful, disgusting, awful*
- opinions expressed indirectly and comparisons with *like*: *People aren't that polite* = People are impolite.
  It's like watching paint dry = It's boring.

3 **A** Read the Skill box and skim the text. Who has a negative opinion about Black Friday? Who enjoys it? Who dislikes it, but always goes?

B Read the second paragraph again and find:

1 three phrases which introduce opinions.   3 an opinion expressed as a comparison with *like*.
2 three adjectives which express opinions.

4 Read the text again. Are the sentences true (T) or false (F)? Correct the false sentences.

1 For Andy, the most important thing about Black Friday is the low prices. _____
2 Andy thinks it's normal for shoppers to behave badly on Black Friday. _____
3 Jen thinks that some people lose control on Black Friday. _____
4 Jen doesn't mind if shoppers are aggressive on Black Friday. _____
5 Chris thinks people save money to buy things they need on Black Friday. _____
6 Chris believes that stores offer fantastic special offers on Black Friday. _____

5 Complete the sentences with *even* or *just*. Scan the text and check.

1 Stores offer huge discounts and special offers for _____ one day.
2 This year was _____ more successful than last year.
3 I got _____ what I wanted.
4 People yell at each other, and there are _____ fights!
5 It seems to me they _____ go crazy when they see a bargain.
6 I'm not _____ sure if the bargains are actually real.

🧩 **Text builder** *even, just*

We use *even* to emphasize surprising information, comparisons, and negatives.
surprise: *I speak French, English, and **even** Chinese.*
comparisons: *His new car is **even** faster than his old one.*
negatives: *He's never **even** heard of my favorite singer!*

We use *just* to mean *only, exactly,* or *simply.*
only: *There's **just** one store on my street.*
exactly: *This shirt is **just** my size.*
simply: *I **just** called to say I love you.*

6 Read the Text builder. What do *even* and *just* mean in the sentences in exercise 5?

7 Do you think big shopping events like Black Friday are a good idea? Why/Why not?

Going CRAZY for a bargain

Black Friday takes place in the U.S. right after Thanksgiving, on the last Friday in November, when stores offer huge discounts and special offers for just one day. It marks the start of the holiday shopping season and takes its name from the fact that this is the first day of the year that stores traditionally start making a profit, going from "in the red" to "in the black." However, the event is now international and more famous for the aggressive behavior of people hunting for low-priced TVs, tablets, and designer clothes. I went to a department store to talk to shoppers about their views on all aspects of the Black Friday phenomenon.

Outside I met Andy, a retired salesclerk, who had lined up all night outside the store to get in first. "Obviously, you can find some amazing discounts," he said, "but if you ask me, the best thing is the experience itself. It's so exciting – camping outside the night before, getting your hands on the latest widescreen TV, reduced from $600 to $249. Personally, I think this year was even more successful than last year – I got just what I wanted," he said, trying to fit two TVs, five

different games consoles, and a vacuum cleaner into his car. I asked Andy about his views on Black Friday's bad reputation. "It doesn't worry me too much. People yell at each other, and there are even fights! But as far as I'm concerned, it's part of the event. If you don't like it, don't come."

Inside the store, Jen, a nurse, was waiting to pay at the checkout. "Every year, I say I'm not going to come, but here I am again," she said with a tired smile. What doesn't she like about it? "People aren't that polite on Black Friday. It seems to me they just go crazy when they see a bargain. And what do we buy? More coffee makers, tablets, stuff we already have, so why are we buying more? I couldn't resist this hairdryer and smartphone today, though, so I suppose I'm part of the problem." She is not a fan of the behavior of some shoppers, however. "It can be chaos, with people kicking and pushing each other out of the way. Sometimes you even see people fighting in front of their kids, and I saw one woman break her wrist as she fell trying to defend her new microwave. To be honest, I find it pretty disgusting."

Finally, I spoke to Chris, a student who had only come into the store to buy a charger for his phone. "I'd forgotten it was Black Friday. I can't believe how many people are here." But aside from that, how does he feel about the day? "From my point of view, it's a terrible idea as it encourages people to be materialistic and spend money on items they can't afford. They pay by credit card and get into debt … it's sad and unnecessary." Chris went on to make the most interesting point I'd heard all day. "I'm not even sure if the bargains are actually real. Some stores seem to increase prices before Black Friday and then lower them, so people think there are huge discounts!" And yet, all over the world, people go crazy for those Black Friday bargains, year after year.

Personal Best   Imagine you were at this department store on Black Friday. Write a short paragraph describing your opinion of it.

5C Tomorrow's world of shopping

1 A Read two people's comments about shopping. Complete the comments with words from the box.

> order   in-store   products   delivery   item   salesclerk

I prefer [1]_____ shopping. It's important to see an [2]_____ before buying it, and to be able to ask a [3]_____ for help or advice.

It's so quick to [4]_____ things online, and home [5]_____ is really convenient. In the future, I think most companies will only sell their [6]_____ online.

B Discuss the questions in pairs.

1 Do you prefer online or in-store shopping? Why?
2 What have you bought in a store recently?
3 What have you bought online recently?
4 How do you think we will shop in the future?

Personal Best

Go to Vocabulary practice: shopping, page 143

2 Read the title of the text. In pairs, discuss what you think is happening in the pictures.

THE **FUTURE** OF SHOPPING

We look at some of the exciting changes that we might see in the not-so-distant future, both in stores and online, but also beyond!

In-store technology

Like in the movie *Minority Report*, face-recognition systems will greet customers by name when they arrive, record what they buy and which parts of the store they spend most time in, and collect information about product preferences by measuring facial expressions. They'll then use all this information to send personalized recommendations and special offers to shoppers' phones while they shop.

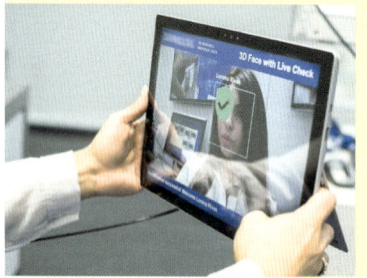

Try before you buy – virtually!

Many clothing stores already have interactive mirrors in the store, which let you try on different clothes virtually at the swipe of a hand. The mirrors use augmented reality to show how the clothes will fit. Similar "magic mirror" app technology is being developed to browse online stores and virtually try on clothes at home, too. We predict that this might be the most popular new technology!

The changing face of stores

Judging by their popularity at present, there are probably going to be more "pop-up" stores – small, temporary stores in places like train stations, parks, or anywhere where there are a lot of people. Meanwhile, many stores may simply stop selling things and become showrooms for companies to display their products. In this way, people will browse in a store and will be able to see and touch the different products, but they will have to order them online.

Neither in-store nor online

As our lives get busier, companies will definitely install more large touch screens in public spaces, where people can browse and order what they want without going to a store. Virtual supermarkets are already available in the subway system in Seoul, South Korea. Passengers order groceries while waiting for their train, and they are delivered to their home the same day.

3 A Read the text. Match 1–5 with a–e to make predictions.

1 In-store technology, such as facial recognition, will
2 Pop-up stores are probably going to
3 People will browse in a store, but buy online and many stores will
4 The writers predict that interactive mirror apps might
5 As our lives get busier, we will definitely

a collect information about our shopping habits and preferences.
b be the most successful new technology.
c see more touch screens in public places.
d appear in more places because they are very popular at the moment.
e stop selling things and become showrooms.

B Which of the shopping predictions do you think are a good idea? Why?

4 Look at the predictions in exercise 3A again. Choose the correct options to complete the rules. Then read the Grammar box.

1 We use *going to* for predictions based on *someone's opinion / present evidence*.
2 We use *will* for predictions based on *someone's opinion / present evidence*.
3 We use *might* and *may* for predictions we are *sure / not sure* about.
4 We use *will definitely* to say that the prediction is more *certain / uncertain*.

 **Grammar** predictions: *will, be going to, may/might*

General predictions:
*I don't think Robert **will** arrive on time.*
*Robots **probably won't** replace humans.*

Predictions based on present evidence:
*She looks like she**'s going to** have her baby very soon!*
*Look at those clouds! It**'s definitely going to** rain.*

Less certain predictions with modal verbs:
*It **may** be cold later. The weather forecast said it's possible.*
*Jill **might** come to dinner. She hasn't confirmed.*

Look! With *will* and *going to*, we can use ***probably*** to make a prediction less certain and ***definitely*** to make it more certain.

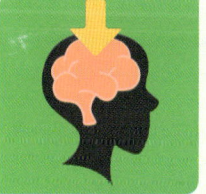 Personal Best

Go to Grammar practice: predictions: *will, be going to, may/might*, page 121

5 A ▶ 5.10 **Pronunciation:** word stress Listen to the sentences and look at the words in **bold**. How many syllables do they have in fast speech? Which syllable is stressed?

1 He'll **probably** be late.
2 I **probably** won't stay awake.
3 It's **definitely** going to be sunny.
4 It's **definitely** not going to snow.
5 She's **probably** going to leave.
6 I'll **definitely** call you.

B ▶ 5.10 Listen again and repeat.

Go to Communication practice: Students A and B page 160

6 Choose the correct options to complete the text.

Experts predict the future – what will the world be like in 2050?

"I think we'll [1]*definitely be / be definitely* able to buy emotions online, upload them to our brains, and we [2]*may be / maybe* able to share them online on social media. If a friend posts a photo of her wedding day, we [3]*will probable / will probably* be able to experience exactly what she was feeling."

"Robots [4]*probably won't / won't probably* only help us with the housework, but they'll also take care of children, and – this is crazy, but possible – they [5]*might / will* even become our closest friends. In the future, this technology [6]*is going to / won't* be much more advanced, and robots and gadgets will sense how we feel and adapt to our emotions."

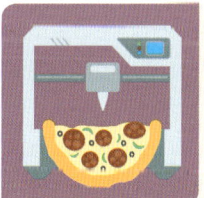

"In 2050, all kitchens [7]*might not / might* have 3D printers that will be able to make dinner. 3D printed pizza, anyone? NASA is already experimenting with 3D printed food for trips to Mars and beyond. If it's successful, technology like this [8]*may / might definitely* help solve the problem of world hunger."

7 In pairs, make predictions about the future. Use some of the ideas below or your own ideas.

| work | pollution | robots | wearable technology | my life | housing |

| space travel | computers | social networks | transportation | food |

I don't think we'll work in offices in the future. We won't need to talk face-to-face with our colleagues as we'll be able to communicate online. What do you think?

Personal Best Complete the following sentences with a prediction: *Next week ..., Next year ..., In five years ... .*

Learning Curve

5D It's not working

1 In pairs, ask and answer the questions.

1 Have you bought anything that you've had to take or send back to the store?
2 What was the problem?
3 Was there a solution? What happened?

2 Look at the picture. What do you think the object in the picture is? What might be the problem with it?

3 ▶ 5.11 Watch or listen to the first part of *Learning Curve*. What is the customer's problem? Choose the correct option.

a He bought the item by mistake.
b The 3D visor he bought isn't working.
c There's something wrong with the video game he bought.

🧩➕ **Conversation builder** | **explaining what's wrong**

Problems with electrical items
I can't get it to work/turn on.
It's not working. / It doesn't work. / It won't work.
It keeps crashing.
There's something missing.
There's something wrong with the ...

Problems with clothes and other items
It's too big/small/tight/baggy.
It doesn't fit.
It's broken/scratched/torn.
It's the wrong size/model/color.
I've changed my mind. I don't want it any more.

---

4 ▶ 5.12 Read the Conversation builder. Complete the customer's description of the problem with the visor. Listen and check.

Customer I bought this visor at a reduced price to use with my video games, and I can't get it to ¹_____ . I'd like to return it.
Marc So what seems to be the problem with it?
Customer It won't, you know, work with the video game. I put it on, and it keeps ²_____ . You know, it just stops ³_____ right away. I think there might be something ⁴_____ in the program or it's just ⁵_____ .

5 In pairs, practice explaining what is wrong with something. Talk about three things each.

6 ▶ 5.13 Watch or listen to the second part of the show. Choose the correct option to answer the questions.

1 At first, what does the customer want Marc to do?
   a exchange the item for the same model
   b exchange the item for a different model
   c give him a refund

2 What happens in the end?
   a Marc fixes the item, and the customer is satisfied.
   b Marc agrees to give the customer a refund, but he can't find his receipt.
   c The customer exchanges the item for a new model.

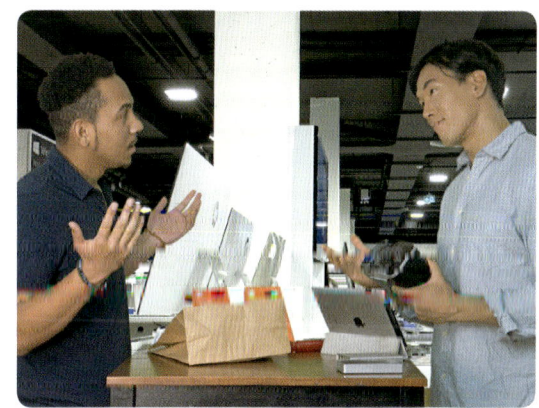

🔧 **Skill** **taking something back to a store**

When you take something back to a store, explain clearly, but politely, what you want.
- Use *I'd like* and *Could I* to sound polite, e.g., *I'd like to exchange it. Could I return it, please?*
- Add phrases like *I think*, *just*, and *if that's possible* to make your request sound less direct. *I'd just like one in a smaller size. I think I'd like a refund, if that's possible.*
- If you're not happy with the proposed solution, explain what you want frankly and firmly, using phrases like *to be honest* and *actually*. *To be honest, I'd just like a refund. Actually, I think I'd prefer a refund.*

7 Read the Skill box. Did the customer explain what he wanted clearly and politely?

8 Order the words to make sentences from the conversation. Who said each sentence, Marc (M) or the customer (C)?

1 to / be / seems / the / what / problem / it / with ? _____
2 return / I'd / to / it / like _____
3 look / take / could / a / I / it / at ? _____
4 honest / I'd / to / be / think / I / like / it / exchange / to _____
5 refund / get / a / please / could / I ? _____
6 I'd / think / I / refund / like / a _____
7 absolutely / need / just / I / see / receipt / to / your _____
8 speak / can / to / manager / your / I / please ? _____

9 Order sentences a–g to make another conversation in a store.

a ☐ **Salesclerk:** Of course. Can I have a look at it?
b ☐ **Customer:** Actually, I'd prefer a refund.
c ☐ 1 **Salesclerk:** Good morning. Can I help you?
d ☐ **Customer:** Yes, sure. Here you are.
e ☐ **Salesclerk:** You're right. There's something wrong with the switch. Would you like to exchange it?
f ☐ **Salesclerk:** No problem. Could I have your receipt and credit card?
g ☐ **Customer:** Hi. I bought this hairdryer yesterday, but it isn't working. Could I return it, please?

Go to Communication practice: Students A and B page 160

10 A **PREPARE** In pairs, prepare a conversation in a store. Decide on:
   - the item
   - the problem
   - what the customer wants
   - what solutions are possible

B **PRACTICE** In pairs, practice the conversation. Take turns being the customer.

C **PERSONAL BEST** Listen to another pair's conversation. Does the customer explain clearly what's wrong? Are both people polite? Can you use something from this conversation in your own? Practice your conversation again.

Work and education

6A Career change

1 In pairs, put phrases a–f in order from 1–6.

a ☐ get a job   c ☐ apply for a job   e ☐ attend an interview
b ☐ get a promotion   d ☐ retire   f ☐ get a degree

Go to Vocabulary practice: work and careers (1), page 144

2 In pairs, discuss your career so far or your hopes for your future career.

3 Read the text quickly. Which two careers has Fabrice Muamba had?

RISING STAR'S CAREER CHANGE

Fabrice Muamba has had an extraordinary life so far. He has lived on two continents and has had two successful careers. He also nearly died on the soccer field in front of a live TV audience of millions. We take a look at his life and his new career.

Fabrice lived in the Democratic Republic of Congo when he was a child, but he has lived in the UK since he was eleven. His career as a soccer player began with a training program at Arsenal Football Club when he was fourteen. Three years later, he finished school and became a full-time professional soccer player. "It was hard, and I had to train every day, but that's how my career really started," he says.

As a professional soccer player, Fabrice was a rising star who scored many goals, signed multimillion dollar contracts, and was frequently named Player of the Season. However, during an important quarter-final game, Muamba's heart stopped, and he collapsed. It was over

an hour before his heart started again, and he was in the hospital for a month. Surprisingly, he made an excellent recovery, but he had to change careers for medical reasons. "I've had to go back to the beginning again with my career, and learn completely new skills," he says, but his new career as a journalist is going well. He has recently completed a degree in sports journalism with a job placement at the BBC, and has already written articles for a national newspaper.

Fabrice has learned a lot from changing careers, and he has become an ambassador for a program called Life Skills, which helps young people prepare for the world of work. So, what advice does he give young people? "I'm really grateful for having so many opportunities and that I've been able to try different things. So that's my main advice: you have to be open to trying lots of new things in order to succeed."

Adapted from theguardian.com

4 A Read the text again. Are the sentences true (T) or false (F)? Correct the false sentences.

1 He **has had** a normal life. _____
2 Fabrice **lived** in the UK when he was a child. _____
3 He **has lived** in the U.S. since he was eleven. _____
4 He **became** a professional soccer player after he finished school. _____
5 He **had** to change careers because of a health problem. _____
6 He **has** recently **completed** a degree in sports journalism. _____
7 He **has** already **written** articles for the BBC. _____
8 In his life, he **has had** a lot of opportunities. _____

B Which verbs in **bold** in 4A are present perfect? Which are simple past?

5 Match the verbs in **bold** in exercise 4A with functions a–e. Then read the Grammar box.

a finished past actions _____ _____ _____
b recently finished past actions _____
c past actions with *already* _____

d life experiences _____ _____
e unfinished past actions
that continue in the present _____

📖 **Grammar** **present perfect and simple past, *already, yet, recently***

Present perfect for past experiences in your life:
I'**ve visited** over 20 countries.
He's never **been** to the U.S.

Present perfect with *already* and *yet*:
She'**s already bought** her ticket.
Have you **read** my e-mail **yet**?

Simple past for finished actions in the past:
I **got** my first job in 2015.   She **lived** here for 10 years.

Present perfect for recent past actions:
I'**ve been tired** lately.
We **haven't seen** Harry *recently*.

Actions that start in the past and continue in the present:
I'**ve studied** English <u>since</u> I was eight years old.
I'**ve known** him <u>for</u> years.

Look! We use *since* with a point in time and *for* with a period of time.

Go to Grammar practice: present perfect and simple past, *already, yet, recently*, page 122

6 A ▶ 6.3 **Pronunciation:** present perfect and simple past Listen to the sentences. Notice the difference between the present perfect and simple past.

1 a I've lived here for five years. b I lived here for five years.
2 a He's met her before. b He met her before.

B ▶ 6.4 Listen and complete the sentences. Which are present perfect? Which are simple past?

1 I _____ him a few times.
2 We _____ our vacation.
3 He _____ a good job.

4 They _____ to take the course.
5 She _____ the company.

7 A ▶ 6.5 Choose the correct options to complete the conversation. Listen and check.

A How long [1]*has Karen been / was Karen* in her current job?
B She [2]*'s been / was* there for a month. She's a project manager in a construction company.
A Was she looking for a job for a long time or [3]*has she gotten / did she get* a job quickly?
B A long time. She [4]*'s been / was* unemployed for two years.
A [5]*Has she done / Did she do* an internship with that company before she got the job?
B No, she didn't. When she [6]*'s applied / applied* for the job, she didn't know the company.
A [7]*Has she ever gotten / Did she ever get* a promotion?
B She got a promotion in her last job, but she [8]*hasn't gotten / didn't get* one on this job yet.
A [9]*Has she taken / Did she take* any training courses recently?
B She [10]*'s taken / took* a project management course when she was unemployed.

B Work in pairs. Ask your partner about a friend or relative who has a job. Use the questions in 7A and your own ideas.

Go to Communication practice: Student A page 160, Student B page 169

8 In pairs, use the prompts to ask and answer the first questions in the present perfect. Then ask for more details in the simple past.

1 how long / live in your house or apartment?   why / move there?   where / live before?
2 see / any good movies recently?   which movie / see?   you / enjoy it?
3 go / on vacation this year?   where / go?   have / a good time?
4 how long / know your newest friend?   how / meet?   where / meet?

Personal **Best** Write four sentences about your life. Use the present perfect and the simple past.

49

6B Dream job

1 Answer the questions in pairs.

   1 Do you know anyone who is doing their dream job?
   2 What kind of work do they do? What does it involve?
   3 Why do they enjoy it?
   4 What would your dream job be?

2 What's the difference between the pairs of words? Discuss in pairs.

   1 job / career   **3** part-time / full-time
   2 employer / employee   **4** CV / application form

Go to Vocabulary practice: work and careers (2), page 144

3 In pairs, make a list of the five most important things you need for job satisfaction.

> 🔧 **Skill**   **understanding specific information**
>
> It's often important to understand specific information and specific words.
> - Read the questions carefully and identify what kind of information you need.
> - Think about the possible words you may hear.
> - Important words are usually stressed in a sentence. *My* **friend**, *who's a* **chef**, *was* **laid off**, *so she* **started** *her own* **business** *making* **wedding cakes**.
> - Try not to confuse similar-sounding words. *He's employed. He's unemployed. She's fourteen. She's forty.*

4 ▶ **6.7** Read the Skill box. Watch or listen to the first part of *Learning Curve*. Make a note of some stressed words you hear for topics 1–4.

1 Penny's current job	
2 Penny's previous job	
3 the study about job satisfaction	
4 temporary job agencies	

5 ▶ **6.7** Watch or listen again. Write one word in each blank to complete the sentences.

   1 Penny finds her current job _____ .
   2 She used to be a _____ assistant.
   3 She found her previous job _____ .
   4 The working conditions in her previous job were _____ .
   5 One study shows that only _____ % of people like their jobs.
   6 Even if their jobs are well-paid, other people feel _____ at work.
   7 Working conditions have changed, and some people don't want a _____ job.
   8 The _____ largest employer in the U.S. is a temp agency.

6 Discuss the questions in pairs.

   1 What are the advantages of having a permanent job? And a temporary job?
   2 Which would you like at this stage in your life? And in the future?

7 ▶ **6.8** Watch or listen to the second part of the show and answer the questions.

1 What's Ira's job?
2 Does he enjoy it?
3 Which job has Kelly applied for?
4 Does she have any experience in that profession?
5 What's Janet's job?
6 Is she working full-time?

8 ▶ **6.8** Watch or listen again. Complete the notes about Ira, Kelly, and Janet with a word or phrase that you hear.

> Ira's responsible for making the store [1]_____ . When he started working there, it was a [2]_____ job. He took over as the manager when his uncle [3]_____ .

> Kelly has sent her [4]_____ , a [5]_____, and a salary request to the TV company. She's also sent them an [6]_____ , and has called them [7]_____ times. Simon recommends asking if she can do an [8]_____ at the company, instead.

> Janet used to work with monkeys, but she got a [9]_____, and now she works with gorillas. She's always wanted to be a [10]_____ .

🧩 **Listening builder**   **sentence stress**

English speakers stress the most important words in a sentence. These are usually words that carry meaning: nouns, adjectives, and verbs. "Grammar" words, such as auxiliaries, prepositions, and pronouns, are often unstressed. There can be one or more unstressed words between the stressed words. The more unstressed words there are between two stressed words, the more quickly they are pronounced.
*I'd **like** to **ask** you about **work**. Do you **have** a **job**?*

9 **A** Read the Listening builder. Look at the stressed words in sentences 1–5. How many unstressed words do you think there are in each blank?

1 _____ hard _____ find _____ dream job.
2 Working conditions nowadays _____ different _____ were _____ past.
3 _____ always known _____ kind _____ job _____ wanted _____ do _____ adult.
4 _____ times _____ call _____ company _____ job interview?
5 _____ more important _____ have _____ well-paid job _____ rewarding job?

B ▶ **6.9** Listen and write the unstressed words in the blanks. Then practice saying the sentences.

10 In pairs, talk about three of the work-related topics below.

> stressful jobs   writing your résumé   job interviews   salaries
> working conditions   rewarding jobs   employers

6C School days

1 In pairs, decide if the words and phrases in the box are positive or negative.

> get into trouble   pass a test   cheat   behave   fail an exam   get good grades

Go to Vocabulary practice: education, page 145

2 Discuss the questions in pairs.

1 Which schools have you been to?
2 Who was your favorite teacher/professor? Why?
3 Did you get into trouble in school? What for?
4 What are your best and worst school memories?

3 Look at the title of the TV show in the preview. In pairs, discuss what you think the show is about. Read the preview and check your ideas.

Are our kids tough enough?
Chinese School

According to the latest research, Chinese children are better than UK children at subjects like math and science. Is this because of the way Chinese students learn? In a fascinating experiment, five teachers come from China to teach a group of teenagers in a UK school for four weeks, using traditional Chinese teaching techniques. At the end of the month, students take exams and compare their grades with the rest of their school year. Which teaching system will get the best grades? Last episode of this three-part series tonight.

4 A ▶ **6.13** Listen to an extract from a radio show about the TV show, *Chinese School*. Complete the notes in the table.

	UK school system	Chinese school system
class size	1 _____ students	2 _____ students
schedule	from 3 _____ a.m. to 4 _____ p.m.	from 5 _____ a.m. to 6 _____ p.m.
method	Students usually ask 7 _____ , discuss their 8 _____ , and do a lot of 9 _____ tasks.	Students listen to the 10 _____ and take 11 _____ . Very 12 _____ teachers.

B Which school system is more similar to your country? Which do you think will get the best grades at the end of the show?

5 A ▶ **6.14** Complete the sentences from the radio show with the words in the box. Then listen and check.

> using   teaching   been   watching   starting   liked

1 Have you been _____ the show over the past few weeks?
2 For the past month, teachers from China have been _____ at a UK school.
3 They've been _____ Chinese teaching techniques.
4 They've been _____ school at 7 a.m.
5 The students haven't _____ this different style of teaching very much.
6 The teachers have _____ very strict.

B Look at the sentences in 5A and answer the questions.

1 Are they finished or unfinished states and actions? (Has the TV show finished?)
2 Which sentences contain action verbs? Which sentences contain state verbs?
3 Look at the action verb sentences. Are they single actions or longer, repeated actions?
4 Do we use *have + been + -ing* with action verbs or state verbs?

6 Read the Grammar box. Which sentences in exercise 5A are in the present perfect continuous and which are in the present perfect?

> 📖 **Grammar** **present perfect continuous and present perfect**
>
> **Present perfect continuous:**
> To emphasize a longer or repeated action over a period of time.
> *I***'ve been waiting** *for you since 3 o'clock!*   *He***'s been coming** *to this English class for three years.*
>
> To talk about a recent past action that has a result in the present.
> *I'm tired because I***'ve been studying** *all day*
>
> **Present perfect:**
> We don't use the present perfect continuous with state verbs – we use the present perfect.
> *I***'ve known** *Laura since we were in elementary school.* NOT ~~*I've been knowing*~~
>
> **Look!** We often use the present perfect continuous to ask and answer questions using *how long*, *for*, and *since*.
> **How long** *have you been studying English?*   *I've been studying English* **for** *ten years/***since** *I was twelve.*

Personal Best

Go to Grammar practice: present perfect continuous and present perfect, page 123

7 Match sentences 1–5 with replies a–e. Then complete the replies with the present perfect continuous or present perfect form of the verbs in the box.

> learn   wait   play   not be   not study

1 Did you know there are no buses today?
2 Have you passed your driving test yet?
3 Why is Jon so tired?
4 Your French isn't very good, is it?
5 What's wrong with Rob?

a No, it isn't. I _____ it for very long.
b Because he _____ basketball all day.
c No, I didn't. I _____ here at the bus stop for ages!
d No, I haven't. I _____ to drive for three years now.
e I'm not sure, but he _____ happy since he failed that exam.

8 A ▶ 6.16 **Pronunciation:** weak form of *been* Listen to replies a–e from exercise 7. Is the word *been* stressed? Does it have a long or short vowel sound?

B ▶ 6.16 Listen, check, and repeat. Then practice questions 1–5 and answers a–e in pairs.

Go to Communication practice: Student A page 160, Student B page 170

9 A When did these things happen in your life? Write something for each category.

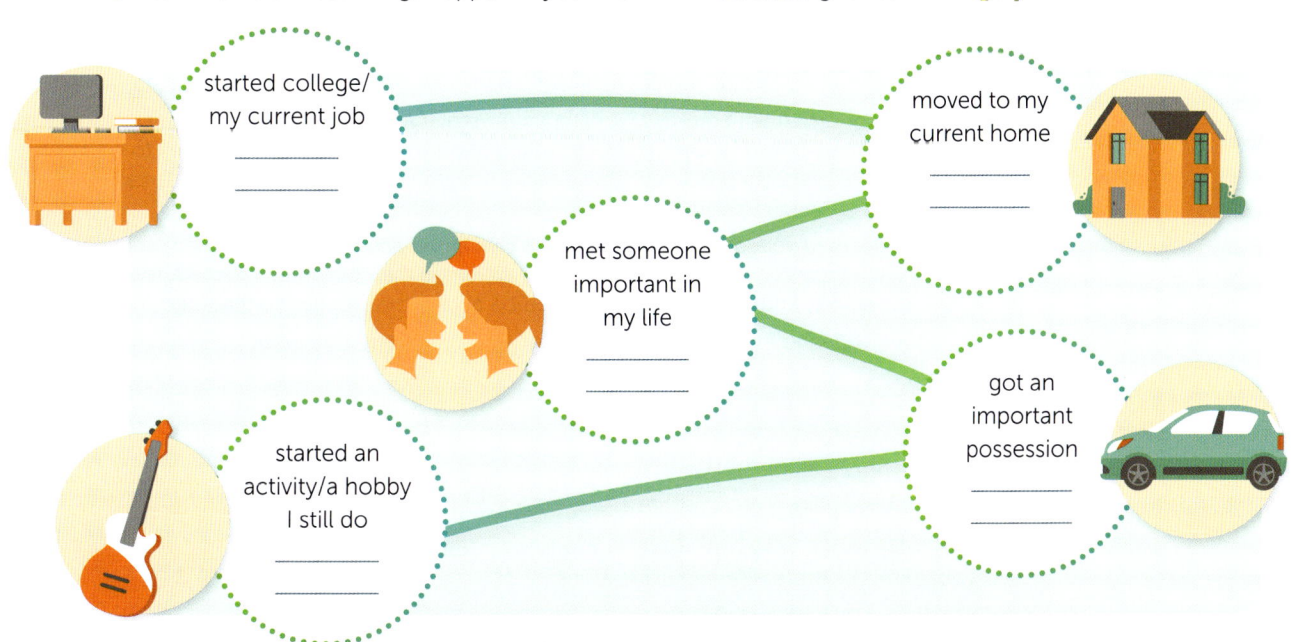

started college/
my current job
_____
_____

moved to my
current home
_____
_____

met someone
important in
my life
_____
_____

got an
important
possession
_____
_____

started an
activity/a hobby
I still do
_____
_____

B Work in pairs. Look at your partner's notes in exercise 9A and ask questions about each event. Include a "How long" question for each event.

Personal Best   Write five sentences with the present perfect or present perfect continuous about your day today.

6D I am writing to apply …

1 Look at the job ad. Would you like to do a job like this? Why/Why not? What skills, qualifications, and experience is the employer looking for?

the La media Factory

Internship at
The L.A. Media Factory

We are looking for an intern to work in our international media center in Los Angeles. The job involves writing articles about the entertainment industry for media organizations around the world. We are particularly interested in recent graduates with some experience in writing.

Candidates should:
- have some experience in digital journalism
- have excellent writing skills
- be highly organized
- have good attention to detail
- work well on a team
- speak English and Spanish fluently.

To apply, please send your CV to Linda Sayer, explaining why you are interested in the position, and providing details of your qualifications, skills, and any relevant experience.

2 Read the cover letter. Does Pablo respond to all the information in the job ad? Is he a good candidate for the job? Why/Why not?

Subject: **Job application – internship position**

Attachment: **CV Pablo Alonso.pdf**

Dear Ms. Sayer:

1 I am writing to apply for the internship position at The L.A. Media Factory, as advertised on internships.com. Please find attached my CV.

2 As you can see from my CV, I have recently completed a degree in Journalism and Media Studies at the University of San Antonio. I believe the skills, experience, and qualities I have developed make me an ideal candidate for the internship position.

3 I am extremely interested in the position because I am passionate about writing and digital media, and I would like to have a career in digital journalism. As part of my degree, I studied areas such as TV and Film Studies, and Digital Journalism. I also completed a six-week job placement, writing short articles for a local newspaper.

4 In addition to my studies, I am currently working as a writer. I am responsible for producing social media posts for a local film society. My work involves writing short movie reviews and guides to increase the film society's social media presence. These tasks require skills such as good organization, time management, and attention to detail.

5 I am a responsible, hardworking person who works well alone and as part of a team. I speak fluent English, and I am a native Spanish speaker. I would welcome the opportunity to work for The L.A. Media Factory, and I am confident I would be a valuable addition to the team.

6 Thank you for considering my application. I look forward to hearing from you.

Sincerely yours,

Pablo Alonso

3 Read the cover letter again. Match sections 1–6 with the information they contain (a–f).

a relevant experience and skills (with specific examples) _____
b relevant academic or professional qualifications _____
c saying which job you're applying for _____
d saying thanks and asking for a response _____
e personal qualities and any additional relevant skills _____
f more relevant experience and skills _____

| **Skill**   **writing a cover letter** |

We write cover letters to introduce ourselves when we apply for a job. We usually send one with our résumé.
- Respond to the information in the job ad. What skills, experience, and qualifications are they looking for?
- Organize your letter so it is brief, easy to read, and makes the employer want to find out more about you.
- Use formal language (*I have been* NOT ~~I've been~~, *I would like* NOT ~~I want~~; *a great deal of* NOT ~~lots of~~).
- Use a formal greeting and ending (*Dear Sir/Madam:* ... *Yours truly*, or *Dear Mr. Smith:* ... *Sincerely yours,*).

4 Read the Skill box. Read sentences 1–8 and <u>underline</u> their formal equivalents in the cover letter.

1 I'm writing because I want the intern job.
2 I think I'm perfect for the job.
3 I really like the job because I like writing.
4 Right now, I work as a writer, too.
5 In this job, I have to write short movie reviews.
6 I need skills like good organization for this job.
7 I really want to work for you. I'd be fantastic!
8 Thanks for your time. Talk soon!

5 Complete the sentences with a preposition. Then check your answers in the cover letter.

1 I am writing to apply _____ the internship position.
2 I have recently completed a degree _____ journalism.
3 I am extremely interested _____ the position.
4 I am responsible _____ producing social media posts.
5 Thank you _____ considering my application.

| **Text builder**   **prepositions after verbs, nouns, and adjectives** |

Some verbs, nouns, and adjectives are followed by a preposition.

Verbs:
*apply **for**, work **as**, look forward **to**,
thank (you) **for***

Nouns:
*a career **in**, a degree **in**,
a certificate **in***

Adjectives:
*ideal **for**, interested **in**,
passionate **about**, responsible **for***

Look! A noun or a verb + *-ing* usually follow these prepositions.
*Thank you for **your e-mail**.   I am looking forward to **hearing** from you.   I'm interested in **taking** a course.*

6 A Read the Text builder. Complete the sentences with a
preposition and information that is true for you.

1 I would like to apply _____ .
2 Eventually, I would like to work _____ .
3 I would like a career _____ .
4 I am passionate _____ .

B Compare your answers in pairs.

7 A | PREPARE | Choose one of the job ads below. Make notes about the skills, qualifications, and relevant
experience to include in your cover letter. Plan how to organize the information.

SUMMER SCHOOL WELCOME STAFF

We are looking for welcome staff to receive and
support our summer school students (aged 14 – 18)
and do administration tasks in our summer school
office. You should have excellent communication
skills, work well on a team, and be able to use Word,
Excel, and Powerpoint. Experience in working with
teenagers a plus.

FASHION BLOGGER

Do you have a passion for fashion? Are you good at
photography? City-based blogger wanted to write
ten blog posts a week for an international lifestyle
website. No professional qualifications required, but
we are looking for someone with good organization
and time-management skills who has experience in
writing a blog.

B | PRACTICE | Write your cover letter. Use formal language and phrases with prepositions.

C | PERSONAL BEST | Exchange letters with a partner. Which job did he/she apply for? Does he/she
respond to everything in the job ad? What do you like best about his/her letter?

Grammar

1 Choose the correct options to complete the sentences.

1 If the bus _____ soon, we'll take a cab.
  a won't arrive   b doesn't arrive   c didn't arrive

2 Look at all this traffic! We _____ be late for our flight.
  a 're going to   b 're going   c won't

3 I _____ in Auckland for five years, from 2008 to 2013.
  a 've lived   b lived   c live

4 I _____ to call her this morning, but there was no answer.
  a 've tried   b tried   c 've been trying

5 We'll go to the park when the rain _____ .
  a is going to stop b will stop   c stops

6 Tom _____ go to the party. He often doesn't go out because he works a lot.
  a will   b 's going to   c might not

7 I _____ to the supermarket today, so you don't need to go shopping.
  a 've already been   b 've been already
  c already gone

8 _____ your best friend since you were in school together?
  a Have you been knowing   b Have you known
  c Did you know

2 Use the words in parentheses to complete the sentences so they mean the same as the first sentence.

1 You'll be late for work if you don't get up now.
  You _____ up now. (won't)

2 It's possible that she'll go to college next year.
  She _____ next year. (may)

3 Julia traveled to Mexico ten days ago, and she's still there.
  Julia _____ ten days. (been)

4 James started that game at two o'clock, and he's still playing it.
  James has _____ two o'clock. (since)

5 I won't go to bed until this movie ends.
  I _____ this movie ends. (as soon as)

6 I'm sure that my team won't lose the game.
  My team _____ the game. (win/definitely)

7 My brother still hasn't learned to drive.
  My brother _____ . (yet)

8 When did you start taking piano lessons?
  _____ taking piano lessons? (how long)

3 Choose the correct options to complete the text.

Companies such as Google and Nissan [1]*conducted / have been conducting* tests on driverless cars for the last ten years. They [2]*have been using / used* powerful computers, which control the speed and direction of the driverless cars automatically. If the tests [3]*will be / are* successful, we [4]*might / won't* see driverless cars on our roads in the next five years. Our technology expert, Dan Jones, gave his opinion of driverless cars: "I think there [5]*won't / will* be far fewer traffic accidents in the future. Unlike humans, computers don't usually make mistakes!"

Dan thinks that driverless cars [6]*won't / will* make driving safer and [7]*can / might* help to reduce traffic congestion. However, if they [8]*will start / start* selling driverless cars in five years, [9]*do / will* drivers want to buy them? Driver Joe Dawson told us what he thinks: "I don't need a driverless car. I [10]*have passed / passed* my driving test in 1992, so [11]*I've been driving / I drive* for over 25 years, and in all that time, [12]*I never have / I've never had* an accident."

Vocabulary

1 Circle the word that is different. Explain your answer.

1 manager   working conditions
  employee   employer

2 delivery   checkout
  career   cart

3 get good grades   look for a job
  do an internship   take a training course

4 graduate   principal
  salesclerk   professor

5 cash   product
  coin   bill

6 permanent   rewarding
  wealthy   part-time

7 CV   salary
  application form   cover letter

8 full-time   nursery school
  term   boarding school

2 Match the words in the box with definitions 1–8.

> browse   professor   reasonable
> waste money on something   be broke
> strict   unemployed   get fired

1 not too expensive _____
2 spend money on something unnecessary _____
3 not have any money _____
4 college or university teacher _____
5 demanding good behavior _____
6 without a job _____
7 look at things you may decide to buy _____
8 do something bad and lose your job _____

3 Choose the correct options to complete the sentences.

1 My bank gave me a $9,000 _____ for a new car.
  a bill   b loan   c borrow
2 When I went to the store, the jeans I wanted were _____ so I couldn't get any.
  a sold out   b paid for   c ordered
3 Gloria _____ her exams because she didn't study.
  a cheated   b failed   c passed
4 When the factory closed, 500 workers _____ .
  a got jobs   b retired   c were laid off
5 I put $75 _____ my savings account every month.
  a by   b into   c for
6 I have to borrow some money _____ my parents to pay for my vacation.
  a from   b for   c of
7 If you do well at work, you might get a _____ .
  a qualification   b good grade   c promotion
8 Sometimes I have to work twelve hours a day, plus weekends! Now I'm looking for a less _____ job.
  a stressful   b rewarding   c varied

4 Put the words in the box under the correct headings.

> return something   do an internship   mortgage
> schedule   employee   taxes   order something online
> take a training course   college   in stock
> special offer   get a degree   ATM   get experience
> savings account   study for

money	shopping

work and careers	education

Personal Best

Lesson 5A
Describe five things you have done with money this week.

Lesson 6A
Describe five things one of your relatives has done in his/her career.

Lesson 5A
Write three sentences: one zero conditional, one first conditional, and one with a future time clause.

Lesson 6A
Write three sentences about your day using the present perfect and *never*, *lately*, and *yet*.

Lesson 5B
Write one sentence with *even* and one with *recently*.

Lesson 6B
Think of three adjectives for a job you would like.

Lesson 5C
Describe three things that happened the last time you went shopping.

Lesson 6C
Name five types of schools.

Lesson 5C
Write three predictions: one with *will*, one with *going to*, and one with *might*.

Lesson 6C
Write three sentences using the present perfect continuous.

Lesson 5D
Give three expressions you can use to explain what's wrong.

Lesson 6D
Name a verb, a noun, and an adjective that are followed by a preposition.

1A Simple present and present continuous; action and state verbs

> ▶ **1.2**
>
> I **check** my e-mails every morning.
> I **need** to access the Internet.
> My sister **has** a new job.
>
> I'**m replying** to your message right now.
> **Are** you **enjoying** your vacation?
> My parents **are having** breakfast.

Simple present

We use the simple present to talk about things that are always true.

They speak Portuguese in Brazil.   The sun sets in the west.

We also use the simple present to talk about regular routines.

I start work at 8:45.   My brother gets up at 6:30 every day.

We often use the simple present with frequency adverbs and expressions.

We never go shopping on Saturdays.   They often go to the beach on the weekend.

Present continuous

We use the present continuous to talk about actions that are happening now.

He's speaking to his sister on Skype right now.   I'm waiting for you at the bus stop.

We also use the present continuous to talk about actions that are temporary.

She's living with her parents at the moment.   I'm studying economics this year.

Action and state verbs

We can use the simple present and present continuous with verbs that describe an action.

I play soccer on Wednesday evenings.
I'm playing a soccer game on my computer right now.

We usually use the simple present, not the present continuous, with verbs which describe a state.

She doesn't like her new haircut. NOT ~~She isn't liking her new haircut.~~
I don't understand. What do you mean? NOT ~~I'm not understanding. What are you meaning?~~
I own a car. NOT ~~I'm owning a car.~~

state verbs	
feelings	*like, love, hate, want, prefer, need* *Enjoy* is used in the continuous tense: *I'm enjoying the party.*
thoughts and opinions	*know, believe, remember, forget, understand, think, feel, consider, realize, expect, agree, suppose, doubt, mean*
states	*be, have (possess), exist, seem, appear, belong, own, matter*
senses	*taste, sound, look, feel, hear, smell*

> **Look!** Some verbs can be both action and state verbs, with different meanings.
> *I'm thinking about my vacation.* (the action of thinking = action verb)
> *I think this website is the best.* (an opinion = state verb)
> *He's having steak and French fries.* (the action of eating = action verb)
> *He has a white sports car.* (a possession = state verb)
> *I'm feeling happy.* (the action of having an emotion = action verb)
> *It feels soft.* (the sense = state verb)

1 Choose the correct options to complete the sentences.

1. They *don't want / aren't wanting* to go swimming today because it's too cold.
2. I *prefer / 'm preferring* this coffee – it *tastes / 's tasting* much better than that coffee.
3. I can't talk to you right now. We *have / 're having* lunch.
4. Why *do you wait / are you waiting* for the bus? There aren't any buses after midnight!
5. I *don't understand / 'm not understanding* this movie because they're speaking too fast.
6. We *think / 're thinking* all museums should be free.
7. He *works / 's working* in the library this morning.
8. That suitcase *belongs / is belonging* to me.

2 Complete the sentences with the simple present or present continuous form of the verbs in parentheses.

1. I _____ (talk) to my boss at the moment. Can I call you back in five minutes?
2. They _____ (send) me a birthday card every year.
3. I _____ (leave) the office now. I'll call you later.
4. You look really tired. I _____ (think) you _____ (need) to go to bed now.
5. I'm so hungry! I _____ (think) about dinner.
6. I can't talk now. I _____ (study) in the library.
7. I _____ (stay) at my best friend's house at the moment.
8. My Internet connection _____ (not work) today.

3 Complete the text with the correct form of the verbs in parentheses.

I [1] _____ (not understand) why some people [2] _____ (believe) that we [3] _____ (talk) to each other much less than in the past. I [4] _____ (own) a smartphone, and I [5] _____ (use) it all the time. I [6] _____ (send) messages to my friends several times a day, and I often [7] _____ (call) them to talk. It's true that we [8] _____ (have) very busy lives nowadays and that we [9] _____ always _____ (not speak) face-to-face. It [10] _____ (seem) to me that electronic devices [11] _____ (make) our lives much easier. For example, I [12] _____ (write) this blog now while I [13] _____ (sit) on the train.

◀ Go back to page 5

1C Question forms

▶ 1.7

Do you **speak** German?
Could we **sit** here, please?
When does class start?

Who told you that story?
How many people work at your company?
What are you **talking about**?

Yes/No questions

To make a question with a *Yes* or *No* answer, we put the verb *be* or an auxiliary or modal verb before the subject. For the simple present and simple past, we use *do/does* and *did*, with the base form of the main verb.

statement	question
He's from the U.S.	Is he from the U.S.?
They've been to China.	Have they been to China?
We were watching TV.	Were you watching TV?
She'll win the game.	Will she win the game?
I can speak Italian.	Can you speak Italian?
They like tea.	Do they like tea?
He plays tennis well.	Does he play tennis well?
We went to Paris.	Did you go to Paris?

Object questions

In most *wh-* questions, the question word or phrase (*who, what, why, how many, what type of*, etc.) is the object of the verb. In object questions, we use an auxiliary verb before the subject, like in *Yes/No* questions.

question word	auxiliary verb	subject	main verb
Where	do	you	live?
Who	did	she	meet?
Why	have	they	come?
What	are	you	doing?
When	will	you	arrive?
How long	can	you	stay?

Subject questions

In subject questions, the question word asks about the subject. We use the affirmative form of the verb, so in present and simple past tenses, we don't use *do/does/did*.

question word	main verb
Who	bought those flowers? NOT ~~Who did buy those flowers?~~
What	happened in 1999? NOT ~~What did happen in 1999?~~
Which animal	makes a noise like that? NOT ~~Which animal does make a noise like that?~~

Questions with prepositions

When the main verb needs a preposition (*look for, talk to, wait for, come from, think about*, etc.), we normally put the preposition at the end of the question.

What are you looking for? NOT ~~For what are you looking?~~
Who was she talking to? NOT ~~To who was she talking?~~
Who did you go to the movies with? NOT ~~With who did you go to the movies?~~

1 Put the words in the correct order to make questions.

1 your friend / work / does / near here / ?
_____

2 like / you / do / going / to concerts / ?
_____

3 was / running / she / why / ?
_____

4 can / tell / you / a secret / I / ?
_____

5 come / from / which / country / you / do / ?
_____

6 speak / more slowly / you / could / ?
_____

7 you / see / did / at the party / who / ?
_____

8 which / to / movie theater / go / you / did / ?
_____

9 from / where / does / he / come / ?
_____

10 looking / who / she / for / was / ?
_____

2 Write subject questions for the statements.

1 Which team _____ ?
Argentina won the game.

2 Who _____ ?
Alexander Graham Bell invented the telephone.

3 How many students _____ ?
More than 40 students study here.

4 What _____ to the phone?
Something strange happened to the phone. Now it's not working.

5 Which movie _____ ?
The movie we saw last week won the Oscar for Best Picture.

6 Who _____ ?
A guy named Jacques lives here.

3 Write questions for the underlined answers.

1 I spoke to Jessica in the park.
_____

2 He gave Mike a book.
_____

3 Carlo and Mira went to the party.
_____

4 We arrived at 4 p.m.
_____

5 The twins drank all the orange juice.
_____

6 She was watching a horror movie.
_____

7 I'm waiting for Toni.
_____

8 Jen works in that building.

◀ Go back to page 9

2A Narrative tenses

 2.2

Last week, we **bought** a new car.
It **was snowing**, and people **were hurrying** home from work.
I **was cooking** dinner when someone **knocked** on the door.
It **had stopped** raining before we **left** the party.
I **was** disappointed because my friends **had forgotten** my birthday.

A narrative describes past events. We often use the simple past, the past continuous, and the past perfect in a narrative.

Simple past

We use the simple past to describe the main events in a narrative. These are completed actions in the past.

Mike opened the door and saw a package on the floor. He picked it up and opened it. He couldn't believe what he saw!

Remember that many simple past verbs are irregular. For a full list of irregular verbs, see page 175.

Past continuous

We use the past continuous to describe the background events in a narrative.

One fall afternoon, I was sitting in the kitchen.
Last night, it was raining, and we were watching TV on the sofa.

We also use the past continuous to describe an action that was in progress when a completed action happened.

She was having breakfast when someone knocked on the door.
I was taking a shower when the phone rang.

We often use *when* and *while* to connect past events.

I was walking along the beach when I found a wallet.
While they were waiting for the bus, it started to rain.

Past perfect

We use the past perfect to describe an action that happened before another action in the past.

I called James at his office, but he had already gone home.
They decided to go for a drive in Paul's new car. He had bought it only two days before.

Look! We can use the three narrative tenses with *when*, with different meanings.
When she arrived, we had dinner. = First she arrived, and then we had dinner.
When she arrived, we were having dinner. = She arrived during dinner.
When she arrived, we had already had dinner. = First we had dinner, and then she arrived.

1 Choose the correct options to complete the sentences.

1 While Tina *rode a bike / was riding a bike* to work, she *was dropping / dropped* her purse.
2 When I closed the door, I *was realizing / realized* that I *left / had left* my keys inside the house.
3 We *watched / were watching* a movie when we *were hearing / heard* a strange noise outside.
4 When John *had gotten / got* home, we told him what *had happened / was happening* earlier that afternoon.
5 When they *were arriving / arrived*, the concert *already began / had already begun*.
6 It was a hot summer's day. We *sat / were sitting* in the garden, and the sun *was shining / shone*.
7 When the movie *was ending / ended*, the children *went / were going* straight to bed.

2 Complete the sentences with the correct past tense of the verbs in parentheses.

1 I _____ (take) my umbrella with me because I _____ (see) the weather forecast earlier.
2 She _____ (read) the whole book while she _____ (wait) for me.
3 While Maria _____ (make) dinner, David _____ (take out) the garbage.
4 I _____ (call) the police right away when I _____ (saw) the broken window.
5 She _____ (start) laughing when she _____ (see) his new hat.
6 I _____ (not want) to see that movie because I _____ (see) it twice before.
7 Anna _____ (live) in San Francisco when she _____ (finish) her first novel.

3 Complete the text with the correct past tense of the verbs in the box.

arrive ring leave put answer walk drive buy

Last Friday, I went to the supermarket to buy a cake for a friend's party. It was really busy as people [1]_____ food for the weekend. While I [2]_____ back to my car, my phone [3]_____. I [4]_____ the cake on the roof of my car and [5]_____ the phone. After the call, I [6]_____ to the party, but I didn't realize that I [7]_____ the cake on my car! Luckily, it was still there when I [8]_____!

◀ Go back to page 13

2C *used to* and *usually*

 **2.11**

My mom **used to have** long hair, but now it's much shorter.
I **didn't use to like** seafood, but now I often eat it.
Did you **use to play** the violin?
I **never used to watch** TV in the evenings.
We **usually** go for a walk after dinner.

used to

We use *used to* + base form to talk about habits or situations that were true in the past, but are not true now. They can be states or actions.

I used to hate classical music, but now I love it. (hate = state)
She used to go swimming every day. (go swimming = action)

We form the negative and questions like other regular verbs in the simple past.

I didn't use to like classical music. NOT *I didn't used to like classical music.*
Did you use to live on this street? NOT *Did you used to live on this street?*

We often use a mixture of *used to* and the simple past when we describe past situations. It sounds unnatural to use *used to* with every verb.

I used to get a lot of exercise when I was in school. I played tennis every weekend, and I went swimming three or four times a week.

We use the simple past, not *used to*, when we talk about things that happened only once, or when we say how many times something happened.

I got a job five years ago. NOT *I used to get a job five years ago.*
We went to Rio three times when I was young. NOT *We used to go to Rio three times when I was young.*

We often use *never used to* instead of *didn't use to*.

He never used to call me but now he calls every day.
The neighbors never used to make so much noise!

usually

Used to only refers to the past. We use *usually* or *normally* + simple present to talk about situations and habits which are true now.

On Sundays, I usually have eggs for breakfast. (present habit)
On Sundays, I used to have eggs for breakfast. (past habit)

> **Look!** We can also use *usually* in the past. It has a similar meaning to *used to*.
> *We usually had dinner together every evening.*
> *We used to have dinner together every evening.*

1 Complete the sentences with the correct form of *used to* or the simple past and the verbs in parentheses. Use *used to* if possible.

1 I _____ my brother and sister regularly, but now we all live in different cities. (see)
2 How _____ to work before you had a car? (you/get)
3 They _____ each other when they were in school, but now they're getting married! (not like)
4 He _____ much money, but now he's rich. (not have)
5 We _____ with our friends more often when we lived in Miami. (get together)
6 Where _____ before you moved here? (you/live)
7 I _____ to reggae music, but now I love it. (never listen)
8 Jon _____ his British friend twice last year. (visit)
9 I used to sing when I was a child, and I _____ the guitar, too. (play)
10 We _____ in Los Angeles in 2012. (get married)

2 Complete the text with *usually* or the correct form of *used to* and a verb from the box.

> not have   go (x2)   arrive   work (x2)

Six months ago, Sarah Thornton left her job in the city and moved to a small town in the country because she wanted a quieter life. "I ¹_____ sixteen hours a day, six days a week," she says. "It was very difficult. I ²_____ home exhausted at around 11 p.m. I ³_____ time for hobbies in the evening, and I didn't see my friends much," she says. "But now I'm happier. I ⁴_____ an eight-hour day now, so I have much more free time. It was strange living in the country at first. In the city, I ⁵_____ to concerts or go shopping on Sundays. There's nothing like that here. Now, I ⁶_____ running or do other outdoor activities every evening."

◀ Go back to page 17

3A Future forms: present continuous, *be going to*, and *will*

▶ 3.4

We**'re taking** the bus to the airport at 6 a.m. tomorrow.
I**'m going to start** learning Japanese this year.
I**'ll make** you a cup of tea, if you want.
I**'ll call** you tonight.
Should we go for a walk?
Should I put some music on?

Present continuous

We use the present continuous to talk about future plans. We usually specify when or where the event will take place.

I'm meeting Sarah at the movies at 8:30 p.m.
We're flying to Miami tomorrow.
They're getting married next year.

We usually use the present continuous to ask people about their plans.

Are you doing anything tomorrow afternoon?
When are you going to the supermarket this week?
What are you doing this weekend?

be going to

We use *be going to* to talk about future plans and intentions.

I'm going to call my mother tonight.
When are you going to buy a new car?

The present continuous and *be going to* have similar meanings, but the present continuous often refers to the more immediate future.

We're going to New York this summer! = It's a definite plan and will happen soon.
We're going to go to New York when we have the money! = It's a plan, but it may be further in the future.

will

We use *will* when we make an offer, promise, or instant decision.

We'll take you to the airport, if you'd like.
I will do the dishes before I go out, I promise!
It's really hot in here. I'll open the window.

Look! We don't use *will* to talk about plans and intentions that are already decided.
I'm going to fly / I'm flying to New York on Tuesday. NOT ~~I'll fly to New York on Tuesday.~~

should

We can use *should* as a question with *I* or *we* to make offers and suggestions.

Should I take you to the airport?
Should we go to that new restaurant by the beach?

1 Choose the correct options to complete the sentences.
   1 Next weekend,
      a we're going to have a party.
      b we'll have a party.
   2 They're staying at a hotel near the beach next week,
      a and they've reserved a room for six nights.
      b but they haven't found a hotel yet.
   3 Oh no, there's coffee all over the floor! Don't worry,
      a I'll clean it up in a minute.
      b I'm cleaning it up in a minute.
   4 He's definitley leaving early tomorrow morning,
      a so he's called a cab for 6 a.m. to go to the station.
      b but maybe he'll stay until lunchtime.
   5 I've made plans to see Sophie next week.
      a We're meeting at 2:30 on Wednesday.
      b We'll meet at 2:30 on Wednesday.

2 Complete the sentences with the present continuous, *be going to*, or *will*. Use the words in parentheses. There may be more than one answer.

   1 I _____ (do) the ironing this week if you want.
   2 We _____ (meet) Linda at 7:30 p.m. at the station. Don't be late!
   3 I'm sorry, but I can't talk now. I _____ (give) you a call when I get home – I promise!
   4 What _____ (you/do) on Saturday? _____ (we/go shopping)?
   5 A Sarah's not here right now. Can I take a message?
      B No, thanks – I _____ (send) her a text.
   6 I've decided I _____ (work) hard next year. I want to get good grades on my exams.
   7 They _____ (arrive) at 11 a.m. – Jack's waiting at the station for them now.
   8 I _____ (get) some exercise this weekend. I might play tennis, or I might go running.
   9 A Do you want a salad or French fries with your hamburger?
      B I _____ (have) French fries, please.
   10 Don't worry – I _____ (not tell) anyone your secret.
   11 Jon wants to live closer to his family, so he _____ (move) in the next few years.
   12 _____ (you/drive) into town later? Can I come with you?

◀ Go back to page 23

3C Defining and non-defining relative clauses

 3.9

That's the man **who lives next door to us**.
That's the couple **that's always arguing**.
She's the woman **whose husband works for the government**.
That's the guy **I sit next to in class**.
My uncle lives in Los Angeles, **which is a really expensive city**.
My neighbors, **who have five children**, are really noisy.

A relative clause gives us more information about the subject of the main clause. We usually start a relative clause with a relative pronoun. We use: .
– *who* or *that* for people
– *that* or *which* for objects
– *whose* + noun for possession
– *where* for places

Defining relative clauses

We use a defining relative clause to say which person, thing, or place we are talking about.

He's the man who I saw yesterday.
That's the phone that I want for my birthday.
She's the girl whose mother is a famous journalist.
That's the restaurant where we had dinner last week.

We can omit *who*, *that*, and *which* when the verbs in the main clause and the relative clause have a different subject.

He's the man (who/that) I met on vacation.
She lost the book (that/which) I lent her.

We can't omit the relative pronoun when it is the subject of the relative clause.

She's the woman who speaks French. NOT ~~She's the woman speaks French.~~

Non-defining relative clauses

A non-defining relative clause gives us extra information about something in the main clause. It doesn't identify what we are talking about. If we omit this clause, the sentence still makes sense.

We add a comma before a non-defining relative clause.

This is my younger brother Ricardo, who lives in Washington D.C.
That's Tony's new sports car, which he bought in London last week.
Right now, Jen's on vacation in São Paulo, where her friend Maria lives.

Sometimes we add a non-defining relative clause in the middle of a sentence. This is more common in written English.

The hotel, which has over 200 rooms, is just 150 m. from the main square.

We can't use *that* in non-defining clauses. We use *who* for people or *which* for things. We can't omit the relative pronoun.

> **Look!** Notice the difference in meaning between the sentences below.
>
> *The students who passed the exam received a certificate.*
> This means that not all the students passed. Only the students who passed received a certificate.
>
> *The students, who passed the exam, received a certificate.*
> This means that all the students passed, and they all received a certificate.

1 A Complete the sentences with the correct relative pronouns.

1 That's the man _____ I spoke to yesterday.
2 The mayor, _____ is in New York for a meeting, didn't answer the journalist's question.
3 It's a story about a man _____ dog saves his life.
4 It's the store _____ we were talking about yesterday.
5 He lives on South Street, _____ is near my office.
6 Michelle's the person _____ normally deals with computer problems.
7 In July, I'm going to stay with my cousin Sara, _____ lives in Mexico.
8 That's the hospital _____ I was born.

B Check (✔) the sentences in A where it's possible to omit the pronoun.

2 Complete the second sentences so they mean the same as the first sentences. Use relative clauses.

1 We went to Bella Pizza. We had lunch there.
We went to Bella Pizza, where we had lunch.
2 Luke gave me a really interesting book yesterday. I'm reading it now.
Luke gave me a really interesting book yesterday, _____
3 Look at that car. My uncle wants one.
Look. That's the car _____ .
4 Can you see the park over there? We're meeting there tomorrow.
That's the park _____ tomorrow.
5 This is Mark. You met his brother last night.
This is Mark, _____ last night.
6 A man left a message for me this morning. What was his name?
What was the name of the man _____ ?

3 Complete the text with phrases a–f and the correct relative pronoun.

a are both younger than me
b we used to do together
c I grew up
d backyard was much bigger
e lived on our street
f I shared with my brothers

My parents still live in the house [1]_____ .
I miss that house. My two brothers, [2]_____
used to annoy me, but I miss some of the things
[3]_____ . I also miss seeing the other kids
[4]_____ . Although it was an old house, it was
really comfortable. My bedroom, [5]_____,
was cool even in the summer. We only had a small
backyard, but we spent a lot of time playing with the boys
next door, [6]_____ than ours.

4A Quantifiers

 4.2

There 's **not much** traffic in my village.   Do you have **a few** minutes to talk?
There are **a lot of** stores in the mall.   I have **no** time to see him today.
There are **too many** buses downtown.
We do**n't** have **enough** places for young people to go.

Small quantities

We use *a little* before uncountable nouns and *a few* before countable nouns.

Can I have a little sugar in my coffee, please?
I'm busy right now. Can I call you back in a few minutes?

We use *not much* and *not many* in negative sentences. We use *not much* before uncountable nouns and *not many* before countable nouns.

There isn't much milk. Can you get some more, please?
I don't have many friends on Facebook.

We also use (very) *little* and *few* (without *a*). They mean *not much* and *not many*.

They speak very little English. = They don't speak much English.
She has very few friends in New York. = She doesn't have many friends in New York.

Large quantities

We use *a lot* (*of*) and *lots* (*of*) in affirmative statements before uncountable and countable nouns. We use *a lot of* before nouns, and *a lot* without a noun.

I have lots of friends in the U.S.   She reads a lot of books. She reads a lot.

We use *plenty of* to say there is enough or more than we need.

Don't worry – we have plenty of time before the train leaves.

> **Look!** In questions, we use *a lot of* before uncountable nouns and *many* or *a lot of* before countable nouns.
> *Was there a lot of snow last year?   Have you invited many people?*

Zero quantity

We use *not any*, *no*, or *none* before uncountable and countable nouns. We use *none* in short answers.

I have no money. = I don't have any money.
There are no tickets left. = There aren't any tickets left.
How many students got 100% on the exam?   None.

More than you need or want

We use *too*, *too many*, and *too much* to mean "more than is necessary or good."

You've put too much sugar in my coffee.
There are too many people on this bus. It's too crowded.

We use *enough* to mean "the right amount" or "sufficient." We can also use *not enough* to mean "less than is necessary" or "less than is good."

I have enough money for a vacation.   There aren't enough parking lots here.

> **Look!** We generally put *enough* before a noun, but after an adjective.
> *There are enough cookies for everyone.* NOT ~~There are cookies enough for everyone.~~
> *The box isn't big enough for all those books* NOT ~~The box isn't enough big for all those books.~~

1 Choose the correct options to complete the sentences.

  1 Riding a bike in New York is dangerous because there are too *many / much* cars on the streets.
  2 Julia has *plenty of / lots* money, so she buys new clothes every week.
  3 There's usually *a lot of / few* snow in Sweden at this time of year.
  4 Do you have *little / a little* free time today so we can have a meeting?
  5 There aren't *enough parks / parks enough* in my town.
  6 Michael's an only child – he has *no / not* brothers or sisters.
  7 *Lots / Much* of my friends are married now, but *a few / a little* are still single.
  8 There isn't *any / no* bread left, so could you get some from the supermarket?
  9 I can't do this crossword – it's *too / too much* difficult for me.
 10 **A** How much ice cream is there in the fridge?
    B *Any. / None.*

2 Read the text. Correct the eight mistakes.

A lot my friends take city vacations, but I can't understand why they want to spend their time off in a city. Most cities are too busy and too noisy. In a crowded city, there isn't space enough because there are always too much people around you. Of course, there are plenty things to buy – but that means that I don't have many money left after spending a little days in a city. I prefer to go to the country or to a beach town, somewhere where there is none traffic and where I can have a few time to myself to think and relax.

◀ Go back to page 31

4C Comparatives and superlatives, *as ... as*

 4.14

My bedroom is **brighter than** the living room.
The first floor apartment is **less expensive than** the second floor apartment.
This is by far **the safest** suburb of the city.
The countryside around here is **the most beautiful** in the whole country.
My house isn't **as big as** my brother's house.

Comparatives

We use comparative adjectives + *than* to compare two things, people, places, etc. With one-syllable adjectives, we add *-er*. With two-syllable adjectives ending in *-y*, we change the *y* to *i* and add *-er*. For adjectives with more than two syllables, we use *more* or *less*.

Her house is smaller than yours.   English is easier than Russian.
Hotels in Tokyo are more expensive than in Madrid./Hotels in Madrid are less expensive than in Tokyo.

We can use *a bit*, *a little*, or *slightly* before a comparative to say there is a small difference, and *a lot*, *much*, or *far* to say there is a big difference.

My new apartment is a bit bigger than my old one.
I'm in much better shape than I used to be.

Superlatives

We use superlative adjectives to say that something is more or less than all the others in a group. With one-syllable adjectives, we put *the* in front and add *-est*. With two-syllable adjectives ending in *-y*, we change the *y* to *i* and add *-est*. With adjectives of more than two syllables, we use *the most* or *the least*.

He's the oldest player on our team.   This is the funniest comedy on TV.
That's the most expensive hotel in Paris./That's the least economical place to stay.

The can be replaced with a possessive adjective.

It's her best album.

We can put *by far* before a superlative to make it stronger.

Lima is by far the biggest city in Peru.

> **Look!** We usually use *in* before places and groups of people, not *of*.
> *She's the best player in the world.   He's the youngest person in my family.*

We often use the superlative with the present perfect + *ever* and *one of the*.

That's the strangest movie I've ever seen.
This is one of the best restaurants in town.

With one-syllable adjectives ending in consonant-vowel-consonant, we double the final consonant and add *-er / -est*.

big – bigger – biggest   hot – hotter – hottest

Some adjectives have irregular comparative and superlative forms.

good – better – best   bad – worse – worst   far – farther/further – farthest/furthest

(not) as ... as

We use *as ... as* to say that two things are the same and *not as ... as* to say that two things are different. We can use *just* with *as ... as* to emphasize a similarity.

Today, Boston is just as warm as Mexico City.
In the winter, Amsterdam isn't as cold as Moscow.

1 Complete the sentences with the words in parentheses. Use the correct form of the adjectives. Add any other words you need.

1 The bed in my hotel room is _____ as my bed at home. (just, comfortable)
2 _____ apartments are downtown. (expensive)
3 Jamie's new car isn't _____ as his old one. (big)
4 Susan lives in one of _____ parts of town. (nice)
5 Learning Spanish isn't as _____ learning Japanese. (difficult)
6 It's one of _____ books I've ever read. (funny)
7 Miami is _____ from New York than from Washington D.C. (a lot, far)
8 In January, Rio de Janeiro is usually _____ Buenos Aires. (slightly, hot)
9 That was _____ game I've ever seen. (by far, bad)
10 Mexican food is _____ British food. (a lot, spicy)

2 Complete the second sentences so they mean the same as the first sentences.

1 John and James are both 1.70 m. tall.
John is _____ James.
2 This restaurant is much better than the others in town.
This is by _____ in town.
3 My new phone was much more expensive than my laptop!
My laptop was _____ expensive _____ my new phone!
4 The class tomorrow starts at 9:10 instead of the usual time of 9:15.
The class tomorrow starts a _____ usual.
5 This is the cheapest watch I could find.
This watch is the _____ expensive I could find.
6 I've never seen a nicer beach before.
This is _____ that I've _____ .
7 His last movie is funnier than this one.
This movie _____ funny as his last one.
8 Jill and Maura are sisters. Maura is 19 and Jill is 18.
Jill is _____ her sister.

5A Zero and first conditional; future time clauses

 5.5

If you **borrow** money, you **need** to pay it back.
If I **ask** my bank manager for a loan, he'**ll say** no.
Tell me **if** you **need** some cash.
You **can't open** an account **unless** you'**re** over eighteen.
I **won't be** able to go shopping **until** I **get** paid this Friday.
I'**ll lend** you some money **after** I **go** to the ATM.

Zero conditional

We use the zero conditional to talk about routines or situations that are generally true, including facts. We use the simple present, in both the *if* clause and the main clause.

If I have time, I normally go for a walk on my lunch break.
I usually ride my bike to work if it's a nice day.
If you heat ice, it melts.

First conditional

We use the first conditional to talk about the result of a possible action. We form the *if* clause with *if* + simple present and we usually form the main clause with *will* + base form.

If we take the bus, we'll get there more quickly.
If John doesn't leave now, he won't get to school on time.
You'll be tired tomorrow if you don't go to bed now.

We can put either clause first with no change in meaning. However, if we put the main clause first, we don't use a comma between the two clauses.

If it's nice this weekend, we'll go camping.
We'll go camping if it's nice this weekend.

We can use the imperative in the main clause.

If you see Matthew tomorrow, tell him about the party.

We can use *unless* to talk about possible future events. It means the same as *if + not*.

Unless you work harder, you won't pass your exams. = If you don't work harder, you won't pass your exams.

Future time clauses

We use the simple present, not *will* + base form, after words and phrases like *when*, *until*, *before*, *after*, and *as soon as* when we are referring to the future.

I'll buy a new phone when this one stops working.
She won't call you back until she finishes her homework.
Before we go out, I'll take a quick shower.
We'll wash the dishes after we have lunch.
I'll call you as soon as we arrive at the airport.

1 Choose the correct options to complete the sentences.

1 You can't come to the party *if / unless* you're invited.
2 I'll call you *until / as soon as* I get my test scores.
3 They'll cancel the flight *if / unless* the weather is bad.
4 I'll get a job *when / until* I finish school.
5 She'll stay with us *until / unless* summer vacation finishes.
6 He'll worry *if / when* you don't call him.

2 Complete the sentences with the correct form of the verbs in parentheses.

1 Plants _____ (die) if they _____ (not get) enough water.
2 If you _____ (not save) money now, you _____ (not have) enough to go on vacation.
3 I think I _____ (get) some coffee before the meeting _____ (start).
4 If I _____ (get) lost when I'm in a foreign city, I usually _____ (ask) someone for directions.
5 I _____ (send) you a text as soon as Helen _____ (arrive).
6 We _____ (not play) tennis unless the weather _____ (improve).
7 My brother _____ (be) excited if his team _____ (win) the game tonight.
8 I _____ (make) dinner after this movie _____ (finish).

3 Complete the ad with the correct form of the verbs in the box.

go   have (x2)   want   not pay
open   be (x2)   prefer   not have

At **MegaBank**, we know that people
¹_____ speaking to a member of staff if they ²_____ questions about their account. But we also understand that if people ³_____ busy lives, they ⁴_____ time to visit or call their bank. That's why **MegaBank** has a new chat app. As soon as you ⁵_____ the app, someone ⁶_____ available to talk to you. If you ⁷_____ to know more, ⁸_____ to our website. You ⁹_____ a penny to download the app if you ¹⁰_____ a **MegaBank** customer!

◀ Go back to page 41

5C Predictions: *will*, *be going to*, *may/might*

 5.9

I'm sure Emily **will love** her present.
I **don't think** we**'ll have** time to go to the museum today.
There are lots of people here. It**'s going to be** a great party!
It **might rain** later this afternoon.
We **may not stay** at home for Thanksgiving this year.

will

We use *will* and *won't* to make predictions about the future, based on our personal opinions. We often use phrases like *In my view/opinion ...* , *I think/feel (that) ...* , *I expect (that) ...,* and *I'm sure (that) ...* before *will* and *won't.*

In my view, Germany will win the next World Cup.
It won't be easy for her to find a cheap apartment in the city.

We often use *Do you think ... ?* to ask someone to make a prediction.

Do you think she'll like her present?

> **Look!** To make a negative prediction with *will*, we normally use the negative form of *think*, followed by *will*.
> *I don't think he'll get the job.* NOT ~~I think he won't get the job.~~

be going to

We use *be going to* to make predictions that we are sure about, based on something we can see or something that we know.

Look at how full the parking lot is. The mall's going to be really busy.
Everyone says Toronto is an amazing city – you're going to have a great vacation.

probably and definitely

We use the adverbs *probably* and *definitely* to make a prediction with *will* or *going to* less certain or more certain.

He'll probably buy a new car next year.
He's probably going to buy a new car next year.
Sarah will definitely go to college.
She's definitely going to go to college.

> **Look!** We use *probably* and *definitely* after *will* but before *won't.*
> *It'll probably rain when we're on vacation.*
> *I definitely won't miss the party.*

may/might

We use *may (not)* or *might (not)* + base form to say that a prediction is possible. They mean "maybe" or "perhaps."

We may not go on vacation this year. = Perhaps we won't go on vacation this year.
It might rain later, so take an umbrella. = Maybe it will rain later, so take an umbrella.

1 Choose the correct options to complete the sentences.

1 Look at those dark clouds. It *will / 's going to* rain!
2 I *'m going to / might* be home before seven, but it depends on the traffic.
3 The score is 10 0! Our team *is going to / will* win the game.
4 Jane *will definitely / definitely will* be at the concert. She bought her ticket months ago.
5 He's studying really hard at the moment. He *might / 's going to* pass the exam easily.
6 I'm sure you *might / 'll* enjoy the movie.
7 It *will / may* snow tonight. There's a 50% chance of snow according to the weather forecast.
8 We're arriving at midnight, so I *think we won't / don't think we'll* have time to go for dinner.
9 She doesn't think they *'ll / won't* move next year.

2 Complete the second sentences so they mean the same as the first sentences. Use the words in parentheses.

1 Perhaps she will win the Olympic gold medal.
  She _____ the Olympic gold medal. (win)
2 I'm absolutely sure that Mark won't pass his driving test.
  Mark _____ his driving test. (fail)
3 We probably won't have time to visit you this month.
  I _____ have time to visit you this month. (think)
4 I'm sure there will be a party this weekend.
  There _____ a party this weekend. (definitely)
5 The weather's awful. Maybe the train will be late.
  The train _____ on time because of the awful weather. (arrive)
6 You'll definitely learn a lot in this course.
  I _____ learn a lot in this course. (sure)
7 It's possible that it will rain later today.
  It _____ later today. (might)
8 We're not going to get to the airport on time with this traffic.
  I _____ get to the airport on time with this traffic. (think)

6A Present perfect and simple past, *already, yet, recently*

> ▶ 6.2
>
> I**'ve never been** fired from a job.
> Ivan **has already finished** work, and it's only 3 p.m.
> I**'ve heard** that Simona is leaving the company.
> My dad **has been** retired **for** twelve years.
> I**'ve been** to Australia twice. I last **went** there two years ago.

Present perfect

We form the present perfect with *have/has* + past participle. We use it:

- to talk about experiences in our lives.
  I've been to the U.S. three times.   I've never eaten Mexican food.
  Have you ever traveled abroad for work?   She's seen this movie before.

- to talk about something that happened earlier than we expected, or didn't happen when we expected, with *already*, *yet*, and *still*.
  I've already spoken to Tony.
  Have you written that report yet?   I haven't finished it yet. / I still haven't finished it.

- to talk about the duration of a situation that started in the past and is still true now, with *for* and *since*.
  I've worked here for ten years.   She's lived here since 1985.

Present perfect or simple past?

We use the present perfect to talk about the past from the perspective of the present.

This is the best book I've ever read. (in my life until now)
I've lived in London for five years. (I still live there.)

In addition to the adverbs above, we often use the present perfect with words and time expressions such as *so far*, *this morning*, *today*, *this week*, and *this year*.

I've seen my friend twice this year.
He's only read one chapter of the book so far.

We use the simple past to talk about completed actions in the past, and <u>when</u> they happened. We often use the simple past with words and past time expressions such as *yesterday*, *last Saturday*, *last week*, *in 2014*, *five years ago*, *What time … ?*, *When … ?*

I lived in London for five years. (I don't live there now.)
We had a great vacation. (We're not on vacation now.)
I read that book last summer.   I got home two hours ago.   When did you arrive?

We use the present perfect or simple past to talk about something that happened a short time ago with *recently*.

We('ve) recently moved to a new office.

We usually use the simple past with just.

I just saw your text message.

Present perfect and simple past

We often ask a question or say something in the present perfect and then give more information in the simple past.

Have you ever met Ana's sister?
Yes, I've met her. I talked to her at Ana's birthday party last month.

Do you know anything about Lima?
Yes, I've been to Lima, so I know it pretty well. I went there last year.

> **Look!** *Ian's been to Lima* means he went to Lima and came back home.

1 Choose the correct options to complete the sentences.

1 I've been to the movies three times *this / last* week.
2 Sarah *has spoken / spoke* to me yesterday.
3 *Have you seen / Do you see* Maria recently?
4 *Do you plan / Have you planned* your vacation yet?
5 *I never went / I've never been* to Moscow.
6 *I've visited / I visited* lots of beautiful places when I was in Argentina last year.
7 This is the most difficult job *I've ever had / I ever had*.
8 Sorry, I *haven't cooked / don't cook* dinner yet. I hope you aren't hungry.
9 Her plane *has arrived / arrived* at 10:45.
10 What *have you thought / did you think* of the movie?

2 Check (✔) the sentences if they are correct. Then correct the incorrect sentences.

1 Tom just moved to Bogotá. _____
2 I've broken my leg six months ago. _____
3 He works here since 2016. _____
4 Michael has worked really hard this year. _____
5 Have you lived here since five years? _____
6 When have they gotten married? _____
7 Have you spoken to Maria about the party yet? _____
8 This is the best pizza I ever had. _____
9 I've seen John in the park yesterday. _____
10 Have you enjoyed the game last night? _____

3 Complete the text with the verbs and adverbs in parentheses. Use the simple past or present perfect.

I love my job. I ¹_____ (be) a wedding photographer for two years. At first it was hard. Photography is a competitive industry, and you need experience. I ²_____ (not get) many assignments in my first year, but recently I ³_____ (become) really busy. I ⁴_____ (already, have) ten weddings this year! I ⁵_____ (work) in a lot of beautiful places – I ⁶_____ (just, do) a wedding at a palace. But things don't always go well. One colleague ⁷_____ (delete) all the wedding photos the day after his first wedding! Another colleague ⁸_____ (still, not receive) the money from a wedding that she ⁹_____ (do) last year. Thankfully, nothing like that ¹⁰_____ (happen) to me yet.

◀ Go back to page 49

6C Present perfect continuous and present perfect

> ▶ 6.15
>
> I**'ve been studying** Spanish **for** 25 years.
> She**'s been playing** tennis **since** 12:30.
> My shirt's dirty because I**'ve been painting** my bedroom.
> I**'ve known** Ed my whole life, but we**'ve** only **been going out** for three months.

Present perfect continuous

We use the present perfect continuous to talk about longer or repeated actions that started in the past and are still true now. We form the present perfect continuous with the auxiliary verb *have* + *been* + *-ing* form of the main verb.

We've been waiting for the bus for 45 minutes.
He's been coming to this restaurant since 2015.

We often use *How long ... ?*, *for*, *since*, and time phrases like *this morning*, *today*, *this month*, *all year* with the present perfect continuous.

How long has she been waiting?
He's been playing that computer game for four hours/since ten o'clock.
I've been taking the bus to work all week because my bike is broken.
Sam's been going to the gym a lot this year.

We also use the present perfect continuous to talk about longer or repeated actions that have recently finished. These actions can have a result in the present.

You look hot! What have you been doing?
I'm hot because I've been sitting in the sun. (result = I'm hot)
The grass is wet because it's been raining. (result = the grass is wet)

Present perfect

We don't use the present perfect continuous with state verbs. To talk about states that started in the past and continue in the present, we use the present perfect.

How long has Matt had his car? NOT ~~How long has Matt been having his car?~~
Matt's had his car since last September. NOT ~~Matt's been having his car since last September.~~
I've known my neighbors for a long time. NOT ~~I've been knowing my neighbors for a long time.~~

> **Look!** We can use both the present perfect and the present perfect continuous with action verbs and *How long ... ?*, *For ...* , and *Since ...* . The meaning is the same.
> *How long have you lived here?*
> *I've lived here since 1980.*
> *How long have you been working here?*
> *I've been working here for seven years.*

1 Complete the sentences with the present perfect continuous form of the verbs in parentheses.

1 James _____ to the gym every day for the last four weeks. (go)

2 How long _____ for that company? (you/work)

3 He _____ much time at home because he's been so busy at work. (not spend)

4 I _____ to this park since I was a child. (come)

5 How long _____ for a cab? (you/wait)

6 What horrible weather! It _____ all morning. (rain)

7 Why do you never answer your phone? I _____ you all evening. (call)

8 You _____ computer games all evening. Go and do your homework now! (play)

2 Choose the correct options to complete the sentences.

1 How long have you *known / been knowing* Anne?

2 *I'm training / I've been training* for the marathon for the last six months.

3 *I've loved / been loving* you since the first time I met you.

4 She's *talking / been talking* on the phone to her boyfriend for over an hour now.

5 Silvia *is doing / has been doing* her homework all morning.

6 I've *owned / been owning* this apartment since 2010.

7 How long *are you coming / have you been coming* to this gym?

8 *We're going / We've been going* to yoga classes for six months.

1A Communication

1 ▶ **1.1** Match phrases 1–10 with definitions a–j. Listen and check.

1 get a text message/an e-mail	_____	**a** send a text message/an e-mail to a person who has sent one to you
2 check your phone	_____	**b** call someone
3 reply to a text message/an e-mail	_____	**c** receive a text message/an e-mail
4 give someone a call	_____	**d** look at your phone to see messages, alerts, etc.
5 share something on social media	_____	**e** give your opinion on something on social media
6 comment on a post	_____	**f** look at a social media/e-mail account to see messages, alerts, etc.
7 check Facebook/your messages	_____	**g** put something on social media, e.g., a photo or video
8 go online/access the Internet	_____	**h** stay in contact with someone
9 keep in touch with someone	_____	**i** have a conversation with someone in person
10 speak to someone face-to-face	_____	**j** connect to the Internet

2 Complete the sentences 1–9 with the words in the box.

> get speak share check reply give keep comment access

1 Sorry, I can't talk now. Can I _____ you a call when I get home?
2 Can I borrow your laptop so I can _____ my messages?
3 I can't _____ the Internet because there's no WiFi here.
4 I had no signal on my phone, so I didn't _____ your text message.
5 My friends often _____ on my blog posts. Sometimes we have long discussions online.
6 It's easy to _____ in touch with your family when you're abroad.
7 I usually _____ my vacation photos on Facebook.
8 It's much better to _____ to someone face-to-face when you have a problem.
9 I didn't _____ to your message because I was in a meeting. Sorry.

◀ Go back to page 4

1C *say*, *tell*, *speak*, and *talk*

1 ▶ **1.4** Complete the chart with *say*, *tell*, *speak*, or *talk*. Listen and check.

1 _____	a language
speak / **2** _____	(to someone) about something quickly/slowly/loudly
3 _____	someone (something) (someone) a lie/the truth/a story/a joke someone a secret
4 _____	hello/goodbye something (to someone) sorry/thanks/congratulations

2 Choose the correct verbs to complete the sentences.

1 Can I *say* / *talk* to Pedro, please?
2 You need to *say* / *tell* sorry to Carl for arriving late.
3 I *told* / *said* her the good news.
4 Mary can *speak* / *talk* two languages.
5 Can I *say* / *tell* you a secret?
6 Sara *said* / *told* something really interesting.
7 Why are you *saying* / *speaking* so loudly?
8 Can you *tell* / *say* me your address, please?

3 Complete the sentences with a form of *say*, *tell*, *speak*, or *talk* and a word or phrase from the box.

> German thanks a secret sorry a great joke to my boss

1 I'm calling to _____ for helping me with my work yesterday.
2 I _____ Jan _____ yesterday. That was a mistake – now everyone knows it!
3 I'm having some problems at work, so I need to _____ .
4 Simon _____ me _____ this morning – it was so funny!
5 I want to learn to _____, so I'm going to take a course at a language school.
6 You were so rude to your brother. I think you should _____ him you're _____ .

◀ Go back to page 8

2A *-ed* and *-ing* adjectives

1 ▶ **2.1** Match the pairs of adjectives with pictures 1–10. Listen and check.

depressed/depressing   excited/exciting   amazed/amazing   amused/amusing   disappointed/disappointing
embarrassed/embarrassing   fascinated/fascinating   annoyed/annoying   terrified/terrifying   shocked/shocking

1 _____

2 _____

3 _____

4 _____

5 _____

6 _____

7 _____

8 _____

9 _____

Wasn't he a cute baby!

10 _____

2 Complete sentences 1–10 with adjectives from exercise 1.

1 I'm really scared of spiders. I find them _____ !
2 My brother always gets home late for dinner, and we all have to wait. It makes me really _____ .
3 Jamie was _____ with his grades – he was hoping to get As, but he only got Cs.
4 I'm watching a really _____ soccer game – the score's 5–5!
5 Sue thought the book about Japanese paintings was _____ . She's really into art.

6 I lost my job, then my girlfriend left me, and now I have no friends. I'm feeling _____ .
7 The people who saw the terrible accident were all _____ .
8 I fell off my chair during the job interview. My face turned bright red, I was so _____ !
9 I was _____ that my boyfriend remembered my mom's birthday because he always forgets important days.
10 Everyone in the theater was laughing, but I didn't find the movie very _____ .

◀ Go back to page 12

2B Phrasal verbs

1 ▶ 2.6 Match sentences 1–9 with pictures a–i. Listen and check.

1 I hate ice skating! I always **fall over**. _____

2 Jack needs to **try on** the jeans before he buys them. _____

3 My best friend wants to **go out** with my brother. She thinks she's in love with him. _____

4 I think my brother would **break up** with her after a few days. He prefers being single. _____

5 **Hurry up**! The bus is coming! _____

6 Ana wants to **sign up** for extra English classes in college. _____

7 Prices will **go up** again next year. _____

8 My neighbors **set off** for Boston early on a long business trip. _____

9 When she got to the checkout, Eva realized she'd **run out** of money. _____

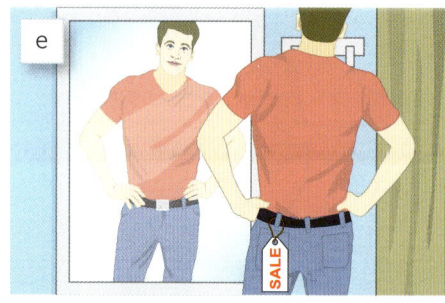

2 ▶ 2.7 Match the phrasal verbs in **bold** with definitions a–f. Listen and check.

1 I'll **pay back** the money my father lent me. _____

2 Jo left her bag at the store, so she has to **go back** to get it. _____

3 It takes a lot of patience and hard work to **bring up** children. _____

4 I haven't seen Alex for ages, but we're going to **catch up** over coffee soon. _____

5 A lot of garbage and plastic bags **end up** in the sea. _____

6 I always **look forward to** my birthday because I enjoy celebrating it. _____

a feel excited about something that is going to happen

b take care of a child until he/she is an adult

c finally be in a place or situation

d meet someone you haven't seen for a while and talk about your news

e return to a place

f return money to the person you borrowed it from

3 Complete the sentences below with the correct form of the phrasal verbs from exercises 1 and 2.

1 The price of a bus ticket _____ by 10% last month.

2 I'd planned to go to the movies with Mark, but he was sick, so I _____ going on my own.

3 My grandparents _____ my cousin after his parents died, and he lived with them until he was 18.

4 My boss is away, but when she gets back, we'll _____, and I'll tell her about the new clients.

5 I stood up very quickly and _____.

6 My colleagues have _____ for an online course in computer programming.

◀ Go back to page 14

3A Personality adjectives

1 ▶ 3.1 Complete sentences 1–9 with the adjectives in the box. Listen and check.

easygoing sensitive reliable helpful organized sensible confident friendly anxious

1 The staff in that store is really _____ . Someone always carries my bags to my car

2 Joe is so _____ . I could never sing in front of so many people, like he does.

3 Mike is very practical and has a lot of common sense. He's so _____ .

4 Tina's always worrying about something. I don't know why she's so _____ .

5 All of Marta's plans for next year are written in her diary. She's very _____ .

6 When Jon says he'll do something, he always does it. He's very _____

7 Ana understands other people's feelings. She's very _____ .

8 The students in my new class took me out for coffee on my first day. They're so _____ .

9 Sarah's always relaxed and calm, and she doesn't worry about things. She's very _____ .

2 ▶ 3.2 Which negative prefix do we use with the adjectives in the box? Put the adjectives in the correct column. Listen and check.

~~kind~~   patient   sensitive   reliable   helpful
polite   friendly   honest   organized   sociable

un-	dis-	im-/in-
unkind		

◀ Go back to page 22

3C Relationships

1 ▶ 3.6 Complete sentences 1–9 with the words and phrases in the box. Use the plural form if necessary. Listen and check.

best friend   close friend   colleague   partner   couple   parents   relative   classmate   next-door neighbor

1 He knows a lot of people here, but he doesn't have many _____ .

2 I went out with some of my _____ from the office after work.

3 That one-bedroom apartment would be perfect for a _____ .

4 I have a lot of _____ who live in the U.S. – mainly cousins.

5 It's not easy these days to find a romantic _____ .

6 I still live with my _____ . It's just me, my mom and my dad.

7 The walls in my building are very thin. I can hear my _____ talking.

8 I've known Liz for ten years. She's the first person I call if I'm sad or if I have good news – she's my _____ .

9 My _____ and I have a WhatsApp group where we talk about our homework.

2 ▶ 3.7 Read sentences 1–8. Match the words and phrases in **bold** with definitions a–h. Listen and check.

1 We had a **falling out** and haven't spoken since.. _____

2 We **argue** a lot because we never agree about what to watch on TV. _____

3 I **get along well** with my neighbors – we're all good friends. _____

4 It's sometimes difficult to **get to know** new people, but I'm lucky – my classmates in college are all really friendly. _____

5 Do you know that girl? Could you **introduce** me to her? _____

6 Sam and Ben had a fight this morning. I told them to **make up**, and now everything's fine! _____

7 It's hard for me to have a conversation with my neighbors since we don't **have a lot in common**. _____

8 I **get together** with my close friends at least once a week. _____

a have a good relationship

b tell someone another person's name when they meet for the first time

c talk to someone in an angry way because you disagree

d meet and go out

e stop being friends with someone because you disagree about something

f have the same interests, experiences, opinions, etc. as someone

g become friends again

h spend time with people so you become friends

◀ Go back to page 26

4A Compound nouns

1 ▶ 4.1 Complete compound nouns 1–12 with the words in the box. Listen and check.

transportation   pedestrian   life   gallery   parking   path   department   jam   shopping   night   sports   town

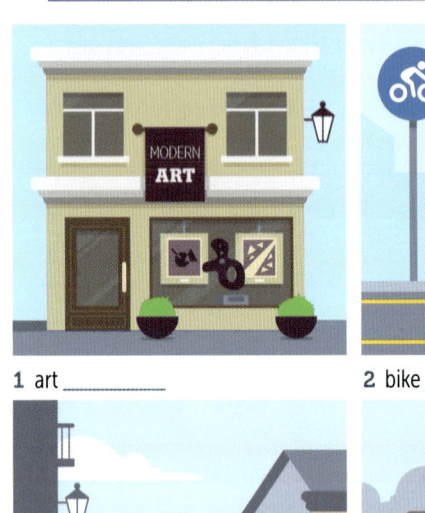

1 art _____

2 bike _____

3 _____ mall

4 _____club

5 _____ area

6 traffic _____

7 _____ lot

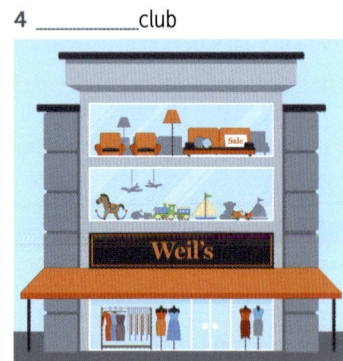

8 _____ store

9 _____ center

10 public _____

11 down_____

12 night_____

2 Complete sentences 1–12 with compound nouns from exercise 1. Use the plural form if necessary.

1 I love shopping in a _____ because you can find so many different things in one store.

2 Let's go to the new _____ near the airport – there are over 300 stores there!

3 I love the _____ in my city. It's great to be able to walk around without any cars.

4 There are lots of _____ in the old part of the city, where you can go dancing until 6 a.m.

5 That _____ has some amazing sculptures and paintings by local artists.

6 I was late for my meeting today. I drove to work, and there was a big _____ .

7 The _____ is great in my city. There are lots of clubs and places to hear music..

8 They've just opened a fantastic new gym at the _____ where I usually play tennis.

9 There aren't many _____ downtown, so it's better to take the bus than to drive.

10 There's a great _____ along the river. It's so relaxing to ride your bike there in the evening.

11 The _____ here is terrible. The buses are dirty, and they're never on time.

12 It's hard to find a good restaurant in my area. The best ones are _____ .

◀ Go back to page 30

4B Common verb phrases

1 ▶ 4.5 Complete diagrams 1–8 with the verbs in the box. Listen and check.

know meet lose miss take catch keep have

someone a lot

a bus

a call

1 _____

a train

coffee

a party

2 _____

a snack

a good time

a train

a class

a bus

3 _____

a cold

a ball

someone for a long time

4 _____

a fact

an exam

a photo

5 _____

someone somewhere

your coat off

weight

your keys

6 _____

a game

touch

in touch

doing something

7 _____

a secret

your promise

someone for the first time

8 _____

a friend for coffee

someone by chance

2 Choose the correct options to complete the text.

I've ¹met / known my friend Carl for ages. We ²met / knew at school when we were kids, but we ³lost / kept in touch for a few years when we went to different colleges. It was my fault. I ⁴took / kept losing my phone, so I ⁵missed / lost all his calls, but he ⁶kept / took calling, and eventually we got together and ⁷had / took coffee together. Since then we've ⁸lost / kept in touch, and we always ⁹have / keep a good time together. He's a great friend.

3 Complete sentences 1–7 with the correct form of the verb phrases in exercise 1.

1 Mark hasn't been eating well in college. Don't you think he's _____ ?

2 My car broke down, and my flight leaves in two hours! Can you _____ airport in your car?

3 I had breakfast ages ago, and I'm a bit hungry. Should we _____ ? I have some cheese and crackers.

4 Jon promised he would come and help me fix my car, but he never came. He didn't _____ .

5 We always _____ when the whole family gets together and put it in the family album.

6 I feel terrible. I have a sore throat and a cough. I think I've _____ .

7 I think I'm going to _____ for my birthday and invite 30 people.

4C Describing homes

1 ▶ 4.9 Match sentence parts 1–10 with a–j. Listen and check.

1 My new apartment has big windows, _____
2 I live in the newest part of the city, _____
3 My best friend's house has a **huge** backyard, _____
4 The windows in my old apartment were **tiny**, _____
5 His old house was **spacious**, but very **basic**; _____
6 My aunt's furniture is all from the 1970s, _____
7 Mike's new apartment is really **convenient** – _____
8 The living room has an open fire, _____
9 Tina's very fashionable, and she's a designer, _____
10 The bed in my hotel room is **comfortable**, _____

a so it was always very **dark**.
b you can walk downtown in ten minutes.
c so it's warm and **cozy** in winter.
d so we often play soccer in it.
e so it's really **bright** during the day.
f so I slept well last night.
g so my apartment is very **modern**.
h so her apartment is full of **stylish** furniture.
i it had five large bedrooms, but no central heating.
j so most of it is very **old-fashioned**.

2 Complete the texts below with the words in **bold** from exercise 1.

Sarah's apartment is only two years old, so it's very ¹_____ . It's a huge apartment – most of the rooms are ²_____, except for the kitchen, which is ³_____, so there's not much space to cook. It's on the top floor, and it has plenty of large windows, so it's very ⁴_____ . She's an architect, so the apartment looks really ⁵_____ . It's only two minutes from the nearest subway station, so it's very ⁶_____ – she can get to work in less than 20 minutes.

My parents live in a ⁷_____ house in the country with six spacious bedrooms. The windows are pretty small, which means it's very ⁸_____ . Also, since they don't have central heating, and there's only one bathroom, it's pretty ⁹_____ . They haven't bought any new furniture for years, so it's pretty ¹⁰_____ . I love their living room; in the winter, they have a real fire, so it's very ¹¹_____ . They also have two old leather sofas that are really ¹²_____ .

3 ▶ 4.10 Complete sentences 1–4 with the words in the box. Listen and check.

> village   suburbs   town   country

1 I live in Melbourne, but my house isn't in the city. I live right outside, in the _____ .
2 I live in a place with a population of about 15,000. I live in a small _____ .
3 There are only a hundred houses where I live. I live in a _____ .
4 Where I live there are farms, fields, and lots of trees. I live in the _____ .

4 ▶ 4.11 Match words and phrases 1–8 with a–h in the picture on the right. Listen and check.

1 apartment building _____
2 basement _____
3 first floor _____
4 second floor _____
5 third floor _____
6 top floor _____
7 balcony _____
8 roof terrace _____

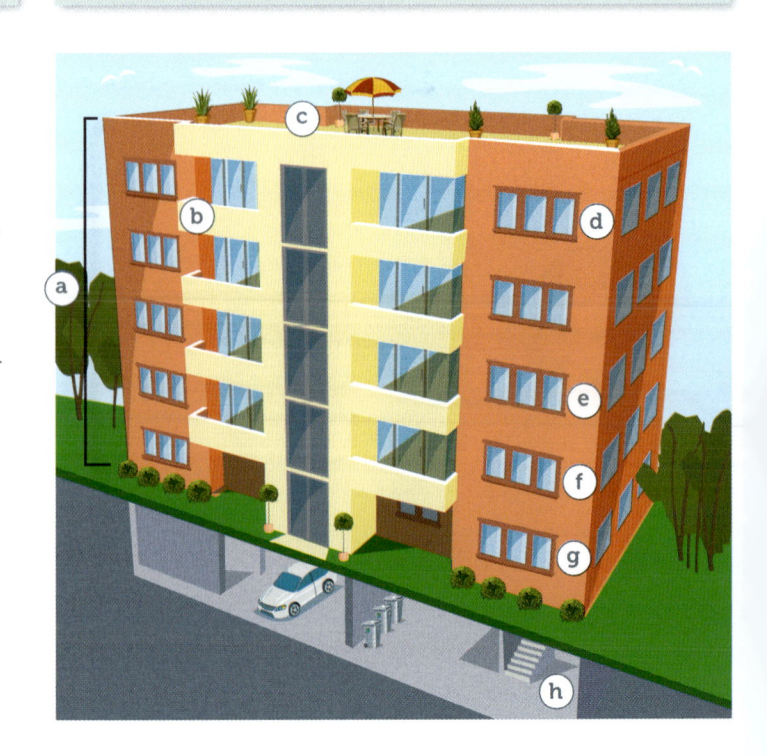

◀ Go back to page 34

5A Money

1 ▶ 5.1 Complete sentences 1–9 with the words in the box. Listen and check.

| credit card wealthy broke coins savings account cash |
| bills loan mortgage taxes ATM save up |

1 The machine at the station didn't accept my _____, so we had to pay with _____ .

2 I want to _____ for a car, so I put $200 into my _____ every month.

3 I needed $100, so I went to the bank. They gave me five $20 _____ .

4 I got a _____ from my bank to buy my car and a _____ to buy my apartment.

5 My uncle's very _____ – he has four houses, six cars, and a boat.

6 I pay a lot of _____ to the government – about 25% of what I earn.

7 In cafés, people normally leave a tip for the waiter. A few _____ are sometimes enough if you only have coffee.

8 Jim realized he was completely _____ – he didn't even have enough money to take the bus home!

9 Can we stop at the _____ ? I need some money.

2 ▶ 5.2 Complete sentences 1–9 with the prepositions in the box. Listen and check.

| on (x2) for by into from out back to |

1 I don't like to **lend** money _____ friends.

2 Can I **pay** _____ credit card?

3 My sister and her husband usually **spend** over $400 _____ clothes every month!

4 How much would you **pay** _____ a second-hand car?

5 I went to the ATM to **take** _____ some money.

6 Can I **borrow** $20 _____ you until tomorrow?

7 Martin shouldn't **waste** so much money _____ lottery tickets.

8 Could you **pay** _____ the money you owe me before the end of the week?

9 I **pay** $50 _____ a savings account for my grandchildren every month.

◀ Go back to page 40

5C Shopping

1 ▶ 5.7 Complete the online product information below with the words and phrases in the box. Listen and check.

| products delivery in stock checkout cart item |

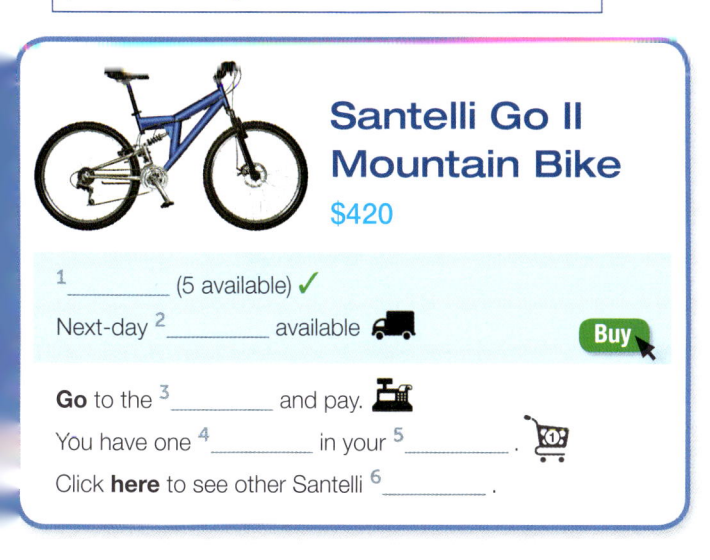

Santelli Go II Mountain Bike
$420

1 _____ (5 available) ✔

Next-day 2 _____ available 🚚 **Buy**

Go to the 3 _____ and pay. 🏪

You have one 4 _____ in your 5 _____ . 🛒

Click **here** to see other Santelli 6 _____ .

2 A Read the review and match words 1–8 with definitions a–h.

I usually prefer ¹**in-store** shopping because I like to ²**browse** different products and see them before I choose what I want. Last month, I went shopping for a new camera. A ³**salesclerk** said there was a ⁴**special offer** on the Cam2. It's a great camera, and at $350 it was very ⁵**reasonable**. I decided to buy one, but it was ⁶**sold out,** so I ⁷**ordered it online**, instead. When the camera arrived, I realized they'd sent me the Cam1 model, instead, so I had to ⁸**return** it.

a no more left to buy _____

b take or send something back _____

c a lower price than normal _____

d bought it on the Internet _____

e a good price _____

f in a store _____

g a person who sells things in a store _____

h look at _____

B ▶ 5.8 Look at the words in **bold** in exercise 2A. Listen and repeat.

◀ Go back to page 44

6A Work and careers (1)

1 ▶ 6.1 Complete sentences 1–11 with the correct form of the words in the box. Listen and check.

be laid off   get a degree   take a training course   get a job
retire   get a promotion   do an internship
resign   look for a job   learn new skills   get experience
get fired   do a job placement

1 Mark is so angry with his boss that he's decided to _____ . He's leaving at the end of the month.
2 Eighty workers _____ at that company last week. They lost their jobs because the company is losing money.
3 Dan _____ from his last job because he was always late.
4 I'm _____ to learn how to use the company's new software.
5 Two years after he joined the company as an assistant manager, Leo _____ . He became the manager.
6 Ed wants to _____ working in a big hotel, so he took a summer job as a receptionist in the largest hotel in Miami.
7 I'd like to _____ when I'm 60 and have a lot of time to enjoy life.
8 Before I can work as a nurse, I need to _____ in nursing, so I'm studying hard, and I hope to get into nursing school in the fall.
9 Sally _____ in a lawyer's office. They didn't pay her a salary, but after six months, they offered her a job.
10 As part of my program, I'm _____ at a design studio. I'm _____ like graphic design.
11 Tim is unemployed, but he is _____ as a salesclerk. I'm sure he'll _____ soon.

2 Choose the correct words to complete the sentences.

1 After she'd been with her company for two years, she got a *job placement / promotion* – she became Sales Manager.
2 Last week, I *took a training course / did an internship* to learn how to use the new database.
3 When the factory closed down last month, all the workers *got fired / were laid off*.
4 She *got fired / resigned* because she stole a computer from the office.
5 My cousin did *an internship / a job* for a year in a television company, but, unfortunately, he didn't get a *promotion / job* at the end of it.
6 Jill has found a new job, so she's *resigned / gotten fired* from her old job.

◀ Go back to page 48

6B Work and careers (2)

1 ▶ 6.6 Match the words in **bold** with definitions a–h. Listen and check.

1 I'm **responsible for** digital marketing.   _____
2 My company was voted the best **employer** in the region.   _____
3 Ian likes traveling. He's had **temporary** jobs in different places.   _____
4 Please send a **cover letter** to introduce yourself and say why you're suitable for the position.   _____
5 I was **unemployed** for a year before I found a job.   _____
6 I work as a waitress, but I'd like a **career** in advertising.   _____
7 They pay my **salary** on the first day of every month.   _____
8 I work with kids. I love seeing them learn. It's very **rewarding**.   _____

a a person or company that employs people
b the occupation you choose for most of your working life
c money you receive for doing your job
d a job that usually lasts a few weeks or months
e a feeling of satisfaction that you've done something useful
f without work
g a document you send with your résumé when you apply for a job
h in charge of

2 Complete the e-mail below with the words and phrases in the box.

full-time   résumé   permanent   application form   well-paid   varied
working conditions   stressful   employees   part-time   manager

● ● ●

When I finished college, I got a ¹_____ job in a restaurant, just a few days a week. This gave me time to finish a project-management course and look for a ²_____ job, not a temporary one. The ³_____ in the restaurant were awful, it was too noisy, and we worked very late. The ⁴_____ was terrible too – he always yelled at us.

I thought an office job would be less ⁵_____, so I sent my ⁶_____ to lots of companies. When I saw an ad for a project manager, I filled in the online ⁷_____ and had an interview. I got the job! I love it. No two days are ever the same. It's very ⁸_____ . It's a small company with only ten ⁹_____ . We all work ¹⁰_____ – 38 hours a week. It's pretty ¹¹_____, so I can save a little money every month.

◀ Go back to page 50

6C Education

1 A Match sentences 1–8 with pictures a–h.

1 **A** Did Sally **get a good grade** on the test?
   B Yes, she got nine out of ten!

2 I have to **hand in** my essay at 8 a.m., not a minute later. My teacher's very **strict**.

3 Gina has started to **study for** her final exams. She's studying all the grammar they've done in class this year.

4 I used to **get into trouble** a lot in school. I didn't **behave** at all. I used to throw things at other students, and I was often sent to the principal's office.

5 You can't **cheat** on the exam. You can't look at your books or ask anyone to help you with the questions.

6 I might **get a degree** in English and French. I'm good at languages, so I think I should study them in college.

7 It's a good idea to **take notes** during lessons and lectures. If you write things down in your notebook, it helps you to remember them.

8 **A** Did you **get your grades** today? Did you **pass** or **fail**?
   B I passed! I got over 60% on all my exams. Sara failed, though.

B ▶ 6.10 Look at the words and phrases in **bold** in 1A. Listen and repeat.

2 ▶ 6.11 Match the words in the box with the definitions. Listen and check.

> principal   term   schedule   professor   graduate

1 part of a school year _____
2 a college teacher _____
3 the manager of a school _____
4 a list of the times and days for classes _____
5 a person who has a college degree _____

3 ▶ 6.12 Complete the chart with the places in the box. Listen and check.

> high school   middle school   nursery school   elementary school
> boarding school   public school   private school

description	place
a school for ages 3–5	1 _____
a school for ages 6–11	2 _____
a school for ages 11–15	3 _____
a school for ages 15–18	4 _____
a school where you don't have to pay	5 _____
a school where you have to pay	6 _____
a school where you study, live, and sleep	7 _____

4 Complete the sentences below with the correct form of a word from exercises 1, 2, or 3.

1 I'm _____ a degree in math. My _____ are all math experts!
2 Private school is very expensive. It's not free like _____ school.
3 I always used to _____ in school. I never _____ into trouble.
4 I can't go out tonight. I have to _____ for an exam tomorrow.
5 You need a degree to apply for that job. It's only for _____ .

a

b

c

d

e

f

g

h

◀ Go back to page 52

145

1A Student A

1 Answer Student B's questions.

2 Ask Student B questions 1–6 using the simple present or present continuous.

1 What / kind / books / you / usually / read?
2 Which books / you / read / at the moment?
3 What / kind / phone / you / have / at the moment?

4 you / have / a good day / today?
5 your classmates / seem / happy / right now?
6 you / own / a pet / at the moment?

1C Student A

1 Read the text quickly. Ask Student B questions to complete the first part of the story. Use the question words in parentheses.

THE TRUTH ABOUT THE LIE:
John and Anne Darwin

One morning in 2002, John Darwin went canoeing
1 _____ (where). That day, the weather was
2 _____ (what like), and the sea was calm, but John
didn't come home. When he didn't go to work, 3 _____
(who) called the police. A few weeks later, 4 _____ (what)
appeared on the beach. Everyone thought John was dead, and
John's wife Anne received 5 _____ (what) because he
had life insurance.

But the story didn't end there because John wasn't really dead. Five
years later, he went 6 _____ (where) and told the police
that he had no memory of the past five years. But they didn't believe
him. So where had he been?

After he disappeared, John hid in the house next door for years. Then
John and Anne bought a house in Panama, and went there. But they
had to go back to the UK to get a new visa – not easy for a dead man,
so John went to the police station saying he had no memory.

However, a journalist found an online photo of the couple, taken in
Panama City in 2006. Soon, everyone found out about their huge lie.
Their children knew nothing about the plan and were very angry. In the
end, John and Anne both went to prison.

2 Answer Student B's questions about the second part of the story.

1D Student A

1 You're on a train. Follow the instructions in the box to make small talk with Student B.

- Greet Student B and ask if you can sit next to him/her.
- Say something about the train.
- Ask him/her where he/she's going.
- Ask what his/her job is.
- Ask what that involves.
- Respond with a positive comment.
- End the conversation and get off the train.

2 You're in a busy café. Student B makes small talk with you. Respond to his/her comments. Use the information in the box to answer his/her questions.

- You live about half an hour outside the city.
- You're a chef at a hotel downtown. You plan menus and create the meals. You really like making bread.
- Your favorite type of cooking is French.

2A Student A

1 Look at the picture and read the story behind it.

What a coincidence!

Neil Douglas, a photographer from Glasgow, was flying to Ireland one night when something very strange happened. He got on the plane and looked for his seat, but he found that a man, Rob Stirling, had already taken it. When Rob looked up at Neil, they were both surprised to see another man with a beard, ginger hair, and blue eyes! Although Neil and Rob are not related, they look exactly like each other. Everyone on the plane was laughing while they took selfies to show their friends.

2 Cover the text and tell Student B the story behind your picture. Use narrative tenses.

3 Look at Student B's picture and listen to the story behind it.

2C Student A

1 Make sentences about Joe using prompts 1–4. Use *used to* and the simple present. Student B listens and corrects.

Five years ago, Joe finished college and got a job in a bank.

In the past	Now
1 Joe / stay in bed / 11 a.m.	he / get up / for work / 6 a.m.
2 Joe / always / wear / casual clothes	he / wear / suit and tie
3 Joe / ride / old bike / to college	he / drive / to work
4 Joe / get / takeout / weekend	he / usually / have dinner / expensive restaurants

2 Read the sentences about Sandra and listen to Student B. Correct Student B's sentences if necessary.

Last year, Sandra won the lottery.

1 Sandra used to live in a small apartment, but now she lives in a huge house with a swimming pool.
2 Sandra didn't use to have a car, but now she usually drives expensive sports cars.
3 Sandra used to be a waitress in a hotel, but now she doesn't work.
4 Sandra used to go to the zoo to see the lions, but now she goes on safaris in Africa.

3A Students A and B

1 Follow the diagram and make plans to do two activities together. Complete the sentences following the prompts in parentheses. Use the activities in the box or your own ideas.

> go to the movies   go out for coffee   have dinner in a restaurant   have a picnic in the park
> go to the beach   go shopping   play tennis   go to a concert

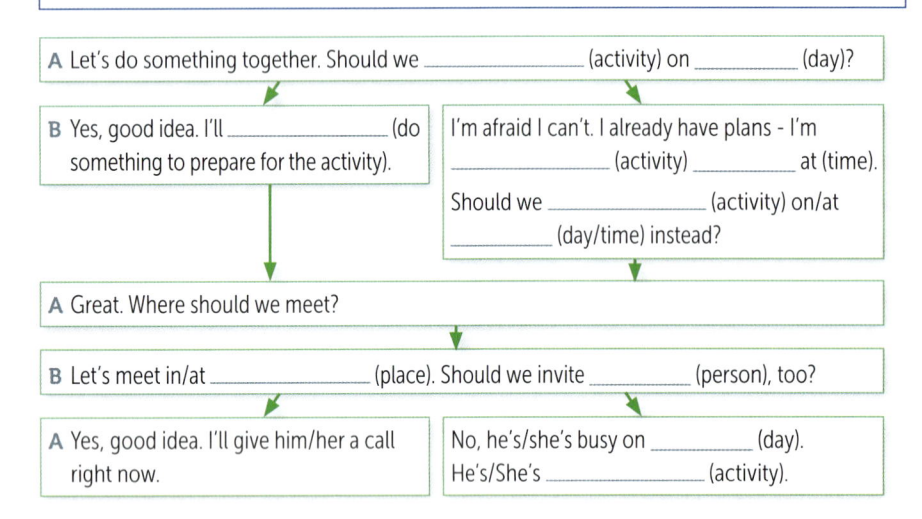

A Let's do something together. Should we _____ (activity) on _____ (day)?

B Yes, good idea. I'll _____ (do something to prepare for the activity).

I'm afraid I can't. I already have plans - I'm _____ (activity) _____ at (time). Should we _____ (activity) on/at _____ (day/time) instead?

A Great. Where should we meet?

B Let's meet in/at _____ (place). Should we invite _____ (person), too?

A Yes, good idea. I'll give him/her a call right now.

No, he's/she's busy on _____ (day). He's/She's _____ (activity).

3C Student A

1 Ask Student B questions 1–5 about his/her neighbor.

  1 Do you have any nice neighbors?
  2 Where's he from?
  3 What does he do?
  4 Is he married?
  5 Do they have any children?

2 Listen to Student B's questions about one of your neighbors. Respond with an answer a–e, completing the sentence with a relative pronoun.

  a He also has a really noisy sports car _____ wakes me up at 5 a.m. every morning.
  b No, he doesn't. He has a teenage son _____'s also very noisy.
  c Because he has to drive to an office 100 km. away, _____ he works as an accountant.
  d Yes, I do. David, _____ lives on the first floor, is really annoying.
  e Well, first of all, he leaves his garbage bags, _____ smell really bad, in front of my door.

3D Student A

1 Tell Student B the three pieces of news in the box. Student B will respond after each piece of news.

  1 I have some good news. I just started my own photography business.
  2 Great news! Remember the exam I failed? Actually, I passed!
  3 I'm afraid I have some bad news for you. You know I'm having financial problems at the moment. Well, I'm sorry, but I can't lend you the money I promised you.

2 Student B will give you three different pieces of news. Listen and respond, using responses a–c.

  a Oh! I'm sorry to hear he's not well. What a shame he can't come!
  b That's wonderful! I'm so happy for you!
  c That's OK. I completely understand.

4A Student A

1 Complete the sentences with *much* or *many*. Then ask Student B the questions.

1 How _____ work do you have at the moment?
2 How _____ coffee do you drink?
3 How _____ free time do you have during the week?
4 How _____ cookies do you eat?
5 How _____ energy do you have on Monday morning?
6 How _____ websites do you usually visit every day?

2 Answer Student B's questions. Use the quantifiers in the box in your answers.

> too much too many (not) enough a lot (of) lots of plenty of
> a little a few not much not many not any no none

4C Student A

1 Look at the information. Ask Student B questions 1–4. Tell Student B if his/her answers are correct.

Buckingham Palace, London
Size: 77,000 sq. m.

Royal Palace, Madrid
Size: 135,000 sq. m.

The White House, Washington, D.C.
Size: 5,000 sq. m.

2 Look at the pictures. Answer Student B's questions.

the cheetah   the kangaroo   the tiger

1 Which building is by far the biggest?
2 Is the White House as big as Buckingham Palace?

Michael Jackson
Record sales: 180 million

Elvis Presley
Record sales: 210 million

Prince
Record sales: 100 million

Mark Zuckerberg, Facebook CEO

Beyoncé, singer

Steven Spielberg, director

3 Who was the most successful singer?
4 Was Michael Jackson slightly more successful or much more successful than Prince?

5A Student A

1 Read sentence parts 1–6 to Student B. He/She will complete them. Decide together if the completed sentences make sense.

1 If I have some money left at the end of this month,
2 If I ask a friend to lend me some money,
3 Should we go out for coffee
4 If we take the bus to the mall,
5 I'll wait here with you
6 Unless I have to work late at the office,

2 Listen to Student B. Complete each sentence part with an ending a–f. Decide together if the completed sentences make sense.

a … we'll arrive at 5 o'clock.
b … I'll go out and celebrate.
c … if you have time.
d … tell her to meet me at the theater.
e … you won't pass the exam.
f … when I get home this evening.

5C Students A and B

1 Look at the chart. Do you think these things will happen in the next ten years? Check (✓) your predictions. Compare your ideas in pairs.

A *I got 99% on my last exam, and I work really hard, so I think I'm going to speak perfect English in the next ten years! What about you?*
B *I don't think I'll speak perfect English in the next ten years. I miss too many classes.*

In the next ten years ...	going to	will definitely	will probably	may/might	probably won't	definitely won't
1 I / speak perfect English						
2 I / run a marathon						
3 I / get married and have children						
4 someone in my family / move to a different city						
5 I / start my own business						
6 computers / replace my English teacher						
7 my country's soccer team / win the World Cup						

5D Students A and B

1 Student A is taking a TV back to the store because the picture isn't clear. Student B is the salesclerk.
Follow the diagram to have a conversation.

Customer (Student A)	Salesclerk (Student B)
Politely get the salesclerk's attention.	→ Offer to help.
Explain the problem with your TV.	→ Offer to check it.
Agree and give the salesclerk the TV.	Confirm that there's something wrong with the screen.
Say that you'd like a refund.	→ Ask for the receipt and his/her credit card.
Give the salesclerk the receipt and card.	→ Confirm that the money is back on the card.

6A Student A

1 Ask Student B the questions in conversations 1–3. Circle his/her answers.

1 Have you ever been to the U.S.?   *yes / no*
   Where did you go?   *New York / Washington, D.C.*
   What was it like?   *great / not great*
2 How long have you been a manager?   *since last year / for a year*
   When did you get a promotion?   *last month / three months ago*
   Have you taken any training courses yet?   *yes / no*
3 You don't look well. What's the matter?   *headache / hurt leg*
   Oh no! How did you do it?   *rollerblading / riding my bike*
   Have you been to see a doctor?   *yes / no*

2 Listen to Student B's questions. Choose the best answer a–c for each question in conversations 1–3.

1 a It was a present from my parents.
   b Yeah, I got it for my birthday.
   c Only for a couple of days.
2 a No, I didn't.
   b Yes, I have.
   c I met the singer Taylor Swift in a restaurant.
3 a He left two minutes ago.
   b To the library, I think.
   c I'm sorry, he just left.

6C Student A

1 Ask Student B questions 1–4.

1 I really like your top. How long have you had it?
2 What's your favorite sports team? How long have you been a fan?
3 Which social networking site do you use the most? How long have you been using it?
4 What TV series are you watching at the moment? How long have you been watching it?

2 Listen to Student B's questions. Respond using the present perfect continuous or the present perfect.

1A Student B

1 Ask Student A questions 1–6 using the simple present or present continuous.

1 What / kind / clothes / you / usually / wear / on the weekend?
2 What / you / wear / today?
3 What / you / think about / right now?

4 What / you / think about / modern art?
5 you / enjoy / studying English?
6 you / enjoy / today's English class?

2 Answer Student A's questions.

1C Student B

1 Read the text quickly. Answer Student A's questions about the first part of the story.

One morning in 2002, John Darwin went canoeing in the sea in the north of England. That day, the weather was good, and the sea was calm, but John didn't come home. When he didn't go to work, John's colleagues called the police. A few weeks later, his broken canoe appeared on the beach. Everyone thought John was dead, and John's wife Anne received a lot of money because he had life insurance.

But the story didn't end there because John wasn't really dead. Five years later, he went to a police station in London and told the police that he had no memory of the past five years. But they didn't believe him. So where had he been?

After he disappeared, John hid [7]_____ (where) for years. Then John and Anne bought [8]_____ (what) in Panama, and went there. But they had to go back to the UK [9]_____ (why) – not easy for a dead man, so John went to the police station saying he had no memory.

However, [10]_____ (who) found an online photo of the couple, taken in Panama City in 2006. Soon, everyone found out about their huge lie. [11]_____ (who) knew nothing about the plan and were very angry. In the end, [12]_____ (what/happen).

THE TRUTH ABOUT THE LIE:
John and Anne Darwin

2 Ask Student A questions to complete the second part of the story. Use the question words in parentheses.

1D Student B

1 You're on a train. Student A makes small talk with you. Respond to his/her comments. Use the information in the box to answer his/her questions.

- You're going for an interview in New York.
- You're an arts administrator. At the moment, you work for a small art gallery, but you'd like to work for a big gallery in New York.
- Your work involves taking care of the gallery's business and planning events. You love modern art and the world of art.

2 You're in a busy café. Follow the instructions in the box to make small talk with Student A.

- Greet Student A and ask if you can sit next to him/her.
- Say something about the café.
- Ask if he/she lives near the café.
- Ask about his/her job.
- Ask another question about his/her job.
- Make a positive comment about something he/she says.
- End the conversation and leave the café.

2A Student B

1 Look at the picture and read the story behind it.

What a coincidence!

In the summer of 2007, Michael Dick, a carpenter from London, was looking for his 31-year-old daughter, Lisa. He had lost touch with her ten years earlier when she had moved to the small town of Sudbury, about 100 km. away. Michael contacted a local newspaper there, and they wrote an article about his search for Lisa. They took a photo of him and his two other daughters. Lisa, who didn't even live in Sudbury any more, saw the newspaper article. She was shocked to see that she was actually in the photo, just a few meters behind her father and sisters!

2 Look at Student A's picture and listen to the story behind it.

3 Cover the text and tell Student A the story behind your picture. Use narrative tenses.

2C Student B

1 Read the sentences about Joe and listen to Student A. Correct Student A's sentences if necessary.

Five years ago, Joe finished college and got a job in a bank.

1 Joe used to stay in bed until 11 a.m., but now he gets up for work at 6 a.m.
2 Joe always used to wear casual clothes, but now he wears a suit and a tie.
3 Joe used to ride an old bike to college, but now he drives to work.
4 Joe used to get takeout on the weekend, but now he usually has dinner at expensive restaurants.

2 Make sentences about Sandra using prompts 1–4. Use *used to* and the simple present. Student A listens and corrects.

Last year, Sandra won the lottery.

In the past	Now
1 Sandra / live / small / apartment	she / live / huge house / swimming pool
2 Sandra / not have / a car	she / usually / drive / expensive / sports cars
3 Sandra / be / waitress / hotel	she / not work
4 Sandra / go / zoo / to see / lions	she / go / on safaris / Africa

3C Student B

1 Listen to Student A's questions about one of your neighbors. Respond with an answer a–e, completing the sentence with a relative pronoun.

a Yes, he is. His wife, _____'s an elementary school teacher, is named Jenny. She's lovely, too.

b Yes, they have a daughter called Tamsin, _____ boyfriend is a professional soccer player.

c Yes, I do. Samuel, _____ lives on the second floor, is really friendly. We get along well.

d He comes from Avalon, _____ is a small town in California.

e He's a computer technician. He works for a company called FIX-IT, _____ repairs computers.

2 Ask Student A questions 1–5 about his/her neighbor.

1 Do you have any bad neighbors?

2 Why is he such a bad neighbor?

3 What else does he do to annoy you?

4 Why does he leave so early?

5 Does he live on his own?

3D Student B

1 Student A will give you three different pieces of news. Listen and respond using responses a–c.

> a That's a relief! Congratulations!
> b Oh. That's a shame. Thank you for telling me.
> c Wow! That's fantastic news!

2 Tell Student A the three pieces of news in the box. Student A will respond after each piece of news.

> 1 I have some bad news. You know my sister just started college. Well, she needs a laptop. I'm afraid I can't give you my old laptop after all. I'm really sorry.
> 2 I have great news! Our restaurant's had an excellent review in a national newspaper!
> 3 I'm afraid I have some bad news about Joe. He needs an operation, so he can't come on vacation with us.

4A Student B

1 Answer Student A's questions. Use the quantifiers in the box in your answers.

> too much   too many   (not) enough   a lot (of)   lots of   plenty of
> a little   a few   not much   not many   not any   no   none

2 Complete the sentences with *much* or *many*. Then ask Student A the questions.

1 How _____ friends do you have on social media?

2 How _____ sleep do you usually get a night?

3 How _____ pairs of shoes do you own?

4 How _____ TV do you watch?

5 How _____ energy do you have on Friday evening?

6 How _____ time do you have to see friends?

4C Student B

1 Look at the pictures. Answer Student A's questions.

The White House, Washington, D.C.

Buckingham Palace, London

Royal Palace, Madrid

2 Look at the information. Ask Student A questions 1–4. Tell Student A if his/her answers are correct.

the tiger
Top speed: 65 km./h

the cheetah
Top speed: 110 km./h

the kangaroo
Top speed: 70 km./h

1 Which is the fastest of the three animals?
2 Is the kangaroo slightly faster or much faster than the tiger?

Prince

Michael Jackson

Elvis Presley

Steven Spielberg, director
Worth: $3.5 billion

Mark Zuckerberg, Facebook CEO
Worth: $55 billion

Beyoncé, singer
Worth: $265 million

3 Who is by far the wealthiest of the three famous people?
4 Is Beyoncé as wealthy as Steven Spielberg?

5A Student B

1 Listen to Student A. Complete each sentence part with an ending a–f. Decide together if the completed sentences make sense.

   a ... I always promise to pay it back immediately.
   b ... when class finishes?
   c ... I'll probably buy some new shoes.
   d ... until the bus comes.
   e ... I'll be home at about 7 o'clock this evening.
   f ... it will be much quicker than walking.

2 Read sentence parts 1–6 to Student A. He/She will complete them. Decide together if the completed sentences make sense.

   1 Unless you study harder,
   2 Come and see me next week
   3 If the train isn't late,
   4 If Kate calls,
   5 As soon as I graduate,
   6 I'll give you a call,

6A Student B

1 Listen to Student A's questions. Choose the best answer a–c for each question in conversations 1–3.

   1 **a** To Washington, D.C.
      b I had a great time.
      c Yes, I went there last year.
   2 **a** About three months ago.
      b Yes, I have – I've been on two courses.
      c Since last year.
   3 **a** I was riding my bike, and I fell off.
      b No, I haven't. It's not that bad.
      c I've hurt my leg.

2 Ask Student A the questions in conversations 1–3. Circle his/her answers.

   1 That's a nice laptop. Is it yours?   *yes / no*
      How long have you had it?   *a short time / a long time*
      Who gave it to you?   *grandparents / parents*
   2 Have you ever met anyone famous?   *yes / no*
      Who did you meet?   *an actor / a singer*
      Did you speak to her?   *yes / no*
   3 Hello. Is Michael there?   *yes / no*
      Do you know where he went?   *to the library / to work*
      When did he leave?   *don't know / two minutes ago*

6C Student B

1 Listen to Student A's questions. Respond using the present perfect continuous or the present perfect.

2 Ask Student A questions 1–4.

1 Why did you decide to learn English? How long have you been learning it?
2 What's your favorite gadget? How long have you had it?
3 What's your favorite singer or band? How long have you been listening to their music?
4 What's your favorite café or restaurant? How long have you been going there?

Infinitive	Simple past	Past participle	Infinitive	Simple past	Past participle
be	was, were	been	lend	lent	lent
beat	beat	beaten	let	let	let
become	became	become	lie	lay	lain
begin	began	begun	lose	lost	lost
bite	bit	bitten	make	made	made
break	broke	broken	mean	meant	meant
bring	brought	brought	meet	met	met
build	built	built	pay	paid	paid
buy	bought	bought	put	put	put
catch	caught	caught	read /riːd/	read /red/	read /red/
choose	chose	chosen	ride	rode	ridden
come	came	come	ring	rang	rung
cost	cost	cost	rise	rose	risen
do	did	done	run	ran	run
draw	drew	drawn	say	said	said
drink	drank	drunk	see	saw	seen
drive	drove	driven	sell	sold	sold
eat	ate	eaten	send	sent	sent
fall	fell	fallen	shut	shut	shut
feel	felt	felt	sing	sang	sung
find	found	found	sit	sat	sat
fly	flew	flown	sleep	slept	slept
forbid	forbade	forbidden	speak	spoke	spoken
forget	forgot	forgotten	spend	spent	spent
forgive	forgave	forgiven	stand	stood	stood
get	got	gotten	steal	stole	stolen
give	gave	given	stick	stuck	stuck
go	went	gone, been	swim	swam	swum
grow	grew	grown	take	took	taken
have	had	had	teach	taught	taught
hear	heard	heard	tell	told	told
hide	hid	hidden	think	thought	thought
hit	hit	hit	throw	threw	thrown
hold	held	held	understand	understood	understood
hurt	hurt	hurt	wake	woke	woken
keep	kept	kept	wear	wore	worn
know	knew	known	win	won	won
leave	left	left	write	wrote	written

Personal
Best

Workbook

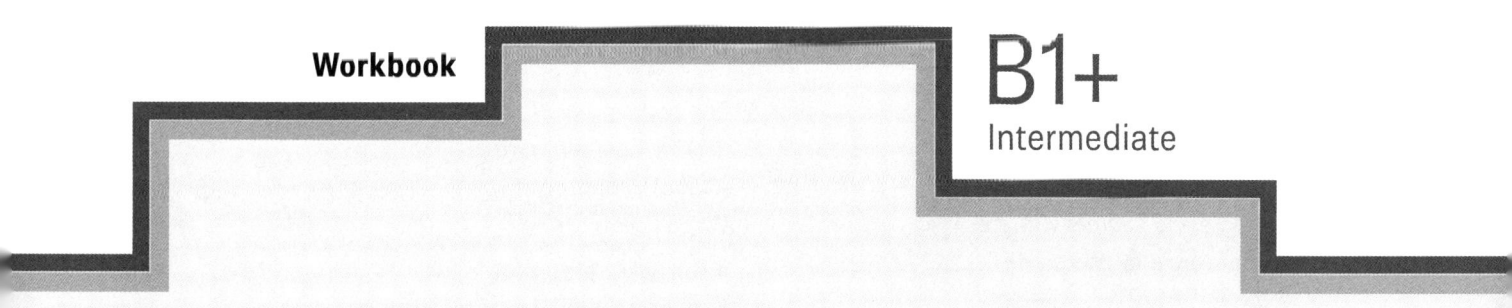

B1+
Intermediate

Richmond

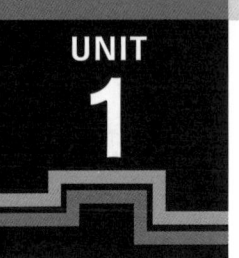

UNIT 1 Communication

1A LANGUAGE

GRAMMAR: Simple present and continuous; action and state verbs

1 Choose the correct words to complete the sentences. Then write A for action verbs and S for state verbs.

1 Look, that's Hugo! *He's coming / He comes* over to see us. _____

2 Should we open the window? *It's feeling / It feels* hot in here. _____

3 I think we should get a bigger TV and Tom *is agreeing / agrees* with me. _____

4 How often *are they going / do they go* to the gym? _____

5 It's great to see you! *Are you having / Do you have* a good time? _____

6 Anna needs some help. She's *not understanding / doesn't understand* what to do. _____

7 My brother *is working / works* in the U.S. at the moment. _____

8 I'm sure that jacket *is belonging / belongs* to Marcia. _____

2 Complete the sentences with the simple present or present continuous form of the verbs in the box. Use two verbs twice.

> have   go   make   think   exist   hate

1 Hannah believes that ghosts really _____.

2 I didn't have time to cook, so we _____ takeout pizza.

3 We _____ to the supermarket once a week.

4 You look happy! What _____ you _____ about?

5 Marco _____ cooking for other people.

6 My sister _____ that I should call our parents more often.

7 _____ you _____ a large apartment?

8 The children _____ a lot of noise because they are very excited.

VOCABULARY: Communication

3 Match the two parts of the sentences.

1 It's very rude to check _____

2 Luckily, he was able to access _____

3 Over 100 people commented _____

4 Michael still keeps _____

5 The couple shared _____

6 I asked Monika to give _____

7 A lot of people go _____

8 When I get _____

a on Suki's latest post.

b in touch with a lot of friends from home.

c me a call later.

d a text message, my phone makes a loud noise.

e online to get medical advice

f the Internet from his hotel room.

g some of their photographs on social media.

h your phone during dinner with friends.

4 Complete the text with the correct words.

> You never see Ethan without his smartphone. He ¹g_____ about 80 text messages a day, and he likes to ²r_____ to them immediately. If you try to ³s_____ to him face-to-face, it can be really annoying because he's always checking his ⁴p_____! He uses Facebook to keep in ⁵t_____ with his friends, and he ⁶c_____ it regularly. He ⁷s_____ lots of photos on it and often ⁸c_____ on his friends' posts. Ethan's parents live in a rural area where it's difficult to ⁹a_____ the Internet, so they don't see his Facebook posts. However, he does ¹⁰g_____ them a call twice a week.

PRONUNCIATION: Sentence stress

5 ▶1.1 Read the sentences. <u>Underline</u> the auxiliary verbs that should be stressed. Listen, check, and repeat.

1 Flora and James are having a party.

2 Does Karl play the piano?

3 Maria isn't feeling very well today.

4 Sasha and Lucia don't want to play tennis.

5 Fatima is studying physics in college.

6 Brett and Owen aren't staying in the same hotel.

7 Ben doesn't have a ticket for the show.

8 Gavin's parents are in Italy.

READING: Skimming a text

Dealing with online trolls

A It's always best to avoid trolls – both the ugly creatures in fairy stories and the equally ugly (on the inside at least) kind who spread their nasty comments by using a computer keyboard. If you look at the comments section of any online newspaper, you will find the second type at work, leaving shocking and unpleasant messages on all sorts of subjects.

B As a society, we value free speech, and, of course, there's a thin line between strong disagreement and messages that are completely unacceptable. But, basically, if someone's main goal is to spread hate and lies, to upset or embarrass someone, or even to scare the person, that person is a troll. Unfortunately, if you use social media, you are sure to have personal experience of trolling sooner or later. Trolls need victims, and they will find them in any online space where people communicate in public.

C If (or when) you meet one, remember that the ability to make you react is like food to a troll – so don't feed them! Trolls are not sensible people. They don't actually want a reasonable discussion, so there's no point at all in trying to have one. It may be tempting to insult or threaten trolls, but they will like this – it is "playing their game," and they are more likely to continue with it than stop. They are only trying to upset you, and if you don't give them a response, they have failed.

D Always remember that the troll is the one with the problem, not you. It's obvious that nobody who hides behind a keyboard to write things he or she would never dare say face-to-face can be a happy and secure person. In fact, newspaper reports of people who have been taken to court for threatening or inappropriate trolling almost always seem to describe sad and lonely lives. Trolls make us furious, but sympathy would probably be a more appropriate emotion.

1 Read the title and look at the pictures. What do you think the article will be about?

- a People who post unpleasant messages online.
- b What to do if your computer is broken.
- c Workers who spend most of their time at a computer.

2 Read the first sentence of each paragraph. Which of A–D do you think will make these points?

1 It's usually best not to reply to trolls. _____
2 We should probably feel sorry for trolls. _____
3 You should try not to have contact with trolls. _____
4 It can sometimes be difficult to decide if someone is actually a troll. _____

3 Read the sentences. Write T for true sentences, F for false sentences, and D when the article doesn't give you enough information to be sure.

1 The word "troll" has more than one meaning. _____
2 Most comments on online newspapers are written by trolls. _____
3 People can sometimes seem rude when they express strong opinions. _____
4 It is possible to use social media sites without seeing messages from trolls. _____
5 Only very intelligent people become trolls. _____
6 Trolls don't like it if you post angry replies. _____
7 Trolls always make a great effort to keep their names secret. _____
8 Trolls are often unhappy people. _____

4 Complete the sentences with your own ideas.

1 I thought Maria was a vegetarian, but, actually,
_____

2 Philippe told everyone he was a pilot, when he was actually
_____

3 Sara's house doesn't have four bedrooms. In fact,
_____

4 I thought polar bears lived in the Antarctic, but, in fact, they
_____

5 I didn't expect Raj to have many Twitter followers, but, in fact,
_____

6 The doctors thought she had the flu, but, actually,
_____

GRAMMAR: Question forms

1 Complete the questions with the words in the box.

> Is   Did   Does   What   Have   Were
> Who   How long   Do   Why

1 _____ you have a good time yesterday evening?

2 _____ did the meeting go on for in the end?

3 _____ should we have for dinner tonight?

4 _____ the city of Tijuana in Mexico or the U.S.?

5 _____ you spoken to Peter at all today?

6 _____ did Liam decide to become a vegetarian?

7 _____ your brother have a job?

8 _____ Alice and Ben pleased when you told them the news?

9 _____ were you talking to when I saw you this morning?

10 _____ you know where the castle is?

2 Complete the questions. Use verbs from the answers in the correct form.

1 A _____ her motorcycle?

B She keeps her motorcycle in the garage.

2 A _____ you for your birthday?

B He gave me a book.

3 A _____ the guitar?

B No, Henry can't play the guitar.

4 A _____ her latest movie yet?

B Yes, I saw it last week.

5 A _____ the concert?

B Yes, I really enjoyed it.

6 A _____ this letter from my bank? It was private.

B I opened it, sorry. I thought it was for me.

7 A _____ Ursula?

B I met her in 2014.

8 A _____ at everyone?

B Paul was yelling because they weren't listening.

9 A _____ you to write that essay?

B It took me three days to write it.

10 A _____ all that noise last night? I couldn't sleep.

B It was the neighbor's cats. I think they were fighting.

VOCABULARY: say, tell, speak, and talk

3 Complete the phrases with *say*, *tell*, *speak*, or *talk*.

1 _____ German

2 _____ goodbye

3 _____ jokes

4 _____ more slowly

5 _____ you're sorry

6 _____ someone a story

7 _____ to someone about a problem

8 _____ the truth

9 _____ that you are hungry

10 _____ thank you

11 _____ someone a secret

12 _____ nice things to someone

4 Complete the sentences with the past simple of *say*, *tell*, or *speak*.

1 Barbara _____ us that she wanted to be alone.

2 I wonder what Pat _____ to Karl to make him so angry?

3 Orla _____ hello and sat down.

4 The man _____ so quietly that nobody could hear him.

5 Michel _____ us a lie, and now we're not friends.

6 Pilar usually _____ English at school and Spanish at home.

7 I'm sure that Matt _____ the police officer the truth.

8 Louis' boss _____ to him about his performance at work.

9 Who _____ congratulations on passing your exams?

10 Leon _____ that the concert is on Saturday night.

PRONUNCIATION: Question intonation

5 ▶1.2 Read the questions. Write (U) if the intonation should go up or (D) for down. Listen, check, and repeat.

1 Do you like cheese? _____

2 Is Gavin coming to the meeting? _____

3 How many brothers and sisters do you have? _____

4 Why is it so dark in here? _____

5 Is this your jacket? _____

6 Where do you come from? _____

7 Which color do you prefer? _____

8 Can you ride a horse? _____

SPEAKING: Making small talk

1 ▶1.3 Rudy, Bella, and Carina meet at a party. Listen to their conversation. Check (✔) the phrases you hear.

1 Is anyone sitting here? _____ _____
2 I don't think we know each other. _____ _____
3 The food's delicious, isn't it? _____ _____
4 I'm a friend of Cristina's. _____ _____
5 Are you from around here? _____ _____
6 So, what do you do for a living? _____ _____
7 And what does that involve? _____ _____
8 Are you having a good time? _____ _____
9 I love your shirt. Is it new? _____ _____
10 Great to meet you. _____ _____
11 Nice talking to you. _____ _____
12 Have a great evening. _____ _____

2 Look at the phrases you checked in exercise 1. Write S if they are used to start a conversation, A if they are used for asking about a person or situation, and F if they are used to end a conversation.

3 ▶1.3 Rudy, Bella, and Carina often give extra information when they answer questions. For each question, identify the main answer and the extra information from a–j. Listen again if you need to.

1 Have you been dancing? Main _____ Extra _____
2 Are you from around here? Main _____ Extra _____
3 So, what do you do for a living? Main _____ Extra _____
4 And what does that involve? Main _____ Extra _____
5 Are you having a good time? Main _____ Extra _____

a Unfortunately, though, I have to be at work at six tomorrow morning, so I need to leave in a minute.
b But I moved back to Quebec.
c Well, I work with people to help them get in shape.
d Yes, I am.
e I love this music.
f I'm a personal trainer.
g I have clients of all ages, from eighteen to 80!
h No, I used to live here.
i I've been doing it for about three years now.
j Yes, for hours!

4 Complete these conversations with your own ideas. Add an extra piece of information to the answer, and then add a positive comment, as in the example.

1 A Are you having a good day?
  B Yes, thanks. *I played tennis this morning, and I won.*
  A *Oh, great! I'd love to play a game with you some time.*
2 A I like your phone. Is it new?
  B Yes, it is. _____.
  A _____.
3 A Do you enjoy classical music?
  B Not really, to be honest.
  _____.
  A _____.
4 A Where do you work?
  B I work downtown.
  _____.
  A _____.

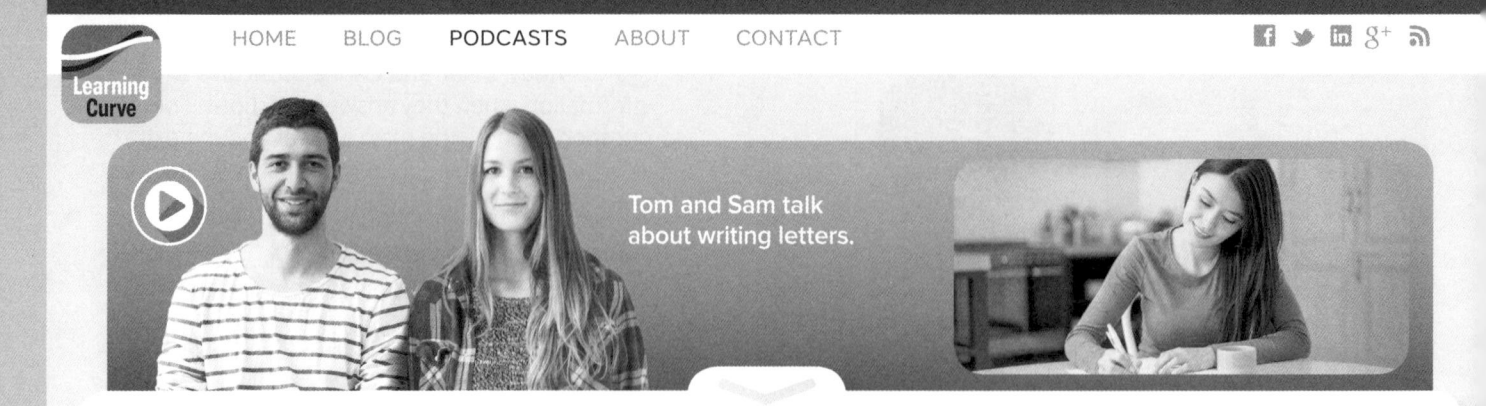

LISTENING

1 ▶ 1.4 Listen to the podcast and choose the best words to complete the sentences.

1 Sophie thinks that we should all *communicate more / write more letters / use social media less*.

2 Sophie believes that writing letters can help people *feel less stressed out / go online less / keep in touch with their family*.

2 ▶ 1.4 Listen again and choose the correct options.

1 Sam asks Tom when he last wrote a letter. What does Tom reply?
   a He can't remember.
   b It was when he was about six.
   c It was about six years ago.

2 How does Sam mainly communicate with her friends?
   a with her phone
   b online
   c with her phone and online

3 According to Sophie, how many teenagers write letters these days?
   a eighteen percent
   b ten percent
   c fourteen percent

4 Tom is surprised that
   a so many young people currently write letters.
   b no young people currently write letters.
   c so few young people currently write letters.

5 Sophie says that when people write to their friends they tell them
   a what has happened in their lives recently.
   b what they think about things.
   c what has happened in their lives and what they think about things.

6 At the end of the interview, Sam says she now wants
   a to write a letter.
   b to receive a letter.
   c someone to write to.

READING

1 Read Penny's blog on page 7 and choose the best summary of her personal challenge last month.

   a to watch what people do when they speak
   b to improve the way she speaks to people
   c to pay more attention to what people tell her

2 Write T for true sentences, F for false sentences, and DS when the writer doesn't say.

1 Penny often blogs about challenges that she has given herself for a month. _____

2 These challenges often involve the person she shares her apartment with. _____

3 Penny is not satisfied with her ability to communicate with other people. _____

4 Penny's roommate knew about Penny's challenge for last month. _____

5 Penny thinks Taylor should try the first point in her plan. _____

6 She made an effort to look at different parts of the speaker's face. _____

7 She says that in our conversations, we should sometimes consider speaking *less*. _____

8 She found it difficult not to look at her phone during the conversations. _____

9 Penny and Taylor had problems in their relationship before Penny started this challenge. _____

10 Taylor noticed their relationship had improved. _____

3 Find seven examples of the verb *tell* in the text.

HOME   BLOG   PODCASTS   ABOUT   CONTACT

Guest blogger Penny tells us how to be a good communicator.

LISTEN AND LEARN!

If you're a regular reader of this blog, you'll be familiar with my 30-day challenges. You'll also know that, although I don't always succeed in these personal challenges, I like to think I learn something along the way. (And you'll probably also know that I have a very patient roommate here – hi, Taylor!)

So are you a good communicator? I like to think I am. I have a wide vocabulary, and I know how to speak to people. What I'm less confident about is my ability to *listen*. So last month's challenge – you guessed it – was to become a better listener. For the last 30 days, when speaking to someone face-to-face, I've followed this four-point plan:

1 Pay attention. Pretend you're going to tell someone else about this conversation in an hour. (This *really* makes you concentrate!)

2 Maintain eye contact. (But don't do this *all* the time – it makes people anxious.)

3 Don't interrupt. (This is a *really* tough one!)

4 Do <u>not</u> check your phone. (Sounds obvious when you read it, right?)

Oh, and in case anyone is wondering, I didn't tell my roommate Taylor at the beginning of the month about my plan to become a better listener. However, I *did* tell her yesterday when I'd finished my challenge. So here's what I learned:

Number 1 *really* works. Honestly – try it! I could probably *still* tell you the details of a conversation I had with Taylor at the start of the month. (Don't worry, Taylor – I'm not telling anyone your secrets here!) This, more than anything, improved my listening skills.

Number 2 is interesting. The idea is to show a polite level of interest by *looking* at the other person when he or she is talking, but not *all the time*. (That would be like an interrogation!) I tried the triangle technique – five seconds looking at each eye, then five seconds at the mouth. It feels strange to begin with, but it allows you to show interest with your eyes without making the other person feel too uncomfortable.

Number 3 is the hardest. The problem is that we *want* to share similar experiences – it's natural. When friends tell us a story about something that happened to them, we want to tell them about a similar thing that happened to us. But sometimes it's better if we just *listen*.

Number 4 wasn't so hard. It's just a bad habit really, and it's impossible to do two things at once!

And did Taylor notice anything different about our conversations? Well, no, she didn't, actually. But, interestingly, she *did* say that she thought we'd gotten along really well recently.

Tell me a story

GRAMMAR: Narrative tenses

1 Choose the correct options to complete the sentences.

1 By the time the doctor _____, Freddie was already feeling better.
   a came   b was coming   c comes

2 When I looked in my bag, I realized that my passport _____.
   a disappeared   b was disappearing
   c had disappeared

3 We prepared the meal together. I cooked the fish, and Tom _____ a salad.
   a made   b was making   c had made

4 When the man _____ her of lying, she became very angry.
   a accused   b was accusing
   c has accused

5 Martha _____ earlier, so we called her to tell her the news.
   a left   b was leaving   c has left

6 Jon and Katie met while they _____ in India.
   a were   b were being   c had been

7 Ollie didn't want to leave the party because he _____ such a great time.
   a had   b was having   c had had

8 I _____ Vera the previous day, so I knew she was in London.
   a saw   b was seeing   c have seen

2 Use the prompts to write sentences with the correct past tenses.

1 Paul/live in Rome/when we meet.
   _____

2 She/not know that/I/guess the truth.
   _____

3 When Colette/show Ben/the photograph/he be/amazed.
   _____

4 Georgia/eat dinner/when Lucy/arrive.
   _____

5 We/get there/at seven but/the others/already go.
   _____

6 They/take/all their furniture so/the room/look very empty.
   _____

7 While Toby/drive to New York/he have/an accident.
   _____

VOCABULARY: -ed and -ing adjectives

3 Match the two parts of the sentences.

1 I hated reading my poems to the class. _____
2 We told the children that we were going to the circus. _____
3 I crashed my parents' car. _____
4 The birds kept trying to steal our food. _____
5 Their boss caught them kissing in the office. _____
6 My grandfather's letters described his adventures in China. _____
7 The rides at the theme park were great. _____
8 Sara and David spent hours visiting the museum. _____

a They were really excited.
b They were extremely annoyed!
c They were absolutely fascinating.
d They were extremely annoying.
e They were so embarrassing!
f They were absolutely fascinated.
g They were really exciting.
h They were so embarrassed!

4 Complete the sentences with -ed or -ing adjectives formed from the verbs in the box.

terrify   annoy   amuse   fascinate   embarrass   excite
amaze   shock   depress   disappoint

1 Rhona's talk was _____ – she made us all laugh.
2 Patrick became _____ after he lost his job.
3 Our plane hit a bad storm – it was absolutely _____.
4 I was _____ to discover that my wallet was missing.
5 It's only a small present – I hope you won't be _____
6 I want to thank my _____ family for their support.
7 Dan is _____ by animals and often visits the zoo.
8 I hardly slept because of an _____ noise.
9 I couldn't remember his name, which was a bit _____.
10 Florian is very _____ about his trip next month.

PRONUNCIATION: /d/ in the past perfect

5 ▶ 2.1 Listen to the sentences. Write 'd if the past perfect is used.

1 I _____ asked Paul to call a taxi.
2 They _____ cooked us a wonderful meal.
3 She _____ thought he was a very interesting man.
4 We _____ worked together in the past.
5 Unfortunately, he _____ heard every word.
6 He _____ tried to give us some advice.

LISTENING: Listening for the main idea

1 ▶2.2 Listen to a conversation between Anna and her friend Enrico. What is the main idea of their conversation?

a Doing things to bring yourself good luck never works.

b Many people do strange things to try to make themselves lucky, and they sometimes work.

c It is important for athletes to do particular things to give themselves luck.

2 ▶2.2 Listen again. Are the following statements true (T) or false (F)?

1 Anna is surprised that Enrico is wearing a yellow tie. _____

2 Enrico wears the yellow tie every day. _____

3 Anna believes the tie will help Enrico pass his driving test. _____

4 Enrico is certain that he wouldn't be successful without his lucky tie. _____

5 Anna's brother's soccer team does not always win when he eats his lucky banana. _____

6 Michael Jordan thought it was lucky to wear the same shorts he wore on his college team. _____

7 Serena Williams never changes her socks. _____

8 Although he is wearing his lucky tie, Enrico is worried about his driving test. _____

3 ▶2.2 Listen to the conversation again. Complete the phrases that the speakers use to talk about doing something in order to be lucky.

1 ... you think that thing's going to _____ a _____?

2 ... this tie always _____ me _____.

3 It's already _____ me _____ my English exam ...

4 ... having a good luck charm really does people _____.

5 I suppose it's because it _____ them _____.

6 ... he thought it _____ his team _____.

7 Does your lucky tie _____ you from getting _____?

4 ▶2.3 Look at these sentences from Anna and Enrico's conversation. Use the mark _ to show where the consonant-vowel links are. Some sentences have more than one link. Listen, check, and repeat.

1 I'm taking my driving test this afternoon.

2 And you think that thing's going to make a difference?

3 I know you like making fun of me.

4 It's already helped me pass my English exam.

5 My brother always eats what he calls his "lucky banana."

6 Athletes seem to do that sort of thing a lot.

7 Does she wash them after each game?

8 It's clearly not just me who has these strange ideas.

5 Complete the sentences with the correct form of the verbs in the box. There are four extra verbs.

> break sign pay look set bring
> go try end hurry fall catch

1 I went to my hometown for the weekend. It was great to _____ up with old friends.

2 We _____ off early on a long drive in order to catch the eight o'clock flight.

3 I had to stop driving because the cost of gas kept _____ up.

4 Harry and Emma went out for three years, but they _____ up when she went abroad to work.

5 Gemma was the nurse who looked after me when I broke my leg, and we _____ up getting married to each other!

6 Don't lend any more money to Jade – you know she'll never _____ you back.

7 We'll miss the train if you don't _____ up!

8 We were in the clothing store for hours. Grace _____ on at least ten dresses!

GRAMMAR: *used to* and *usually*

1 Complete the sentences with *used to, use to,* or *usually.*

1 When Joe was younger, he _____ go to a country school.
2 Our family didn't _____ have a car.
3 My father _____ came home from work at six.
4 The horses _____ slept in their stable at night.
5 Grandma _____ get angry if we were late for dinner.
6 Did Joe _____ live in the U.S.?
7 Hamida didn't _____ be so adventurous.
8 Did Miriam _____ have long hair?
9 Our family _____ went to Italy in summer.
10 My parents _____ grow all their own vegetables years ago.

2 Complete the sentences with the correct form of the verbs in the box. Use *used to* where possible.

| be let help meet not have not get |
| watch go babysit not like |

1 When I was younger, I _____ to the movies at least once a week.
2 _____ Gina _____ on the same hockey team as you?
3 Luiza _____ Petar three years ago, I think.
4 Laura's family _____ a television.
5 I _____ cheese, but I absolutely love it now!
6 We always _____ my brother with his homework.
7 Arjun _____ the game on TV last night.
8 _____ your parents _____ you stay out late when you were a teenager?
9 Henry often _____ for his little sister.
10 Andrew and Lottie _____ any exercise at all.

3 Complete the conversation with *usually* or the correct form of *used to* and the verbs in parentheses. Some items have two answers.

A This is the house where we ¹_____ (live) when I was little. I ²_____ (share) a bedroom with both of my sisters.
B Wow, three of you in one room!
A Yes. People ³_____ (not live) in such small houses nowadays, do they? But my parents didn't mind. My mom ⁴_____ (say) that more rooms just meant more housework for her to do!
B That's one way to look at it, I suppose! But I think people ⁵_____ (prefer) bigger houses because they're more comfortable, don't you?
A ⁶_____ (share) a room with your brothers?
B Yes, I did. Mom ⁷_____ (get) really annoyed with us because we stayed up so late, talking and laughing. And then we ⁸_____ (fall) asleep in class and get into trouble!
A You were lucky! My sisters ⁹_____ (not talk) to me very much – they were much older than me. But I ¹⁰_____ (not mind), though. I was happy reading my books.

PRONUNCIATION: Sentence stress

4 ▶2.4 Read the sentences and underline the syllables you think will be stressed. Listen and check.

1 I used to love her visits.
2 Did Rod use to play with you?
3 We didn't use to watch TV.
4 Did Katie use to help you?
5 Megan didn't use to come with us.
6 The teachers used to yell a lot.
7 Zoe used to play the piano.
8 Lucas didn't use to ride a bike.
9 Did your teacher use to be late a lot?
10 Maria didn't use to like swimming.

WRITING: Making a narrative interesting

COINCIDENCE IN CAIRO

I had become fascinated with Egypt <u>after</u> spending hours in the Egyptian section of our local museum. As a child, I always wanted to go there. However, my parents weren't thrilled with the idea, so I had to wait <u>until</u> I could afford to pay for the trip myself.

To be honest, I'd almost forgotten about it, but then my friend Angela mentioned that her sister was working in Egypt. [1]_____ So last summer I decided to go there on vacation. I bought a plane ticket from Chicago to Cairo and reserved a hotel downtown that Angela had recommended.

<u>As soon as</u> I arrived, I went straight to the tourist office and reserved a place on a tour of the great Pyramids. [2]_____ I turned to look at the person next to me, to see if he or she was as amazed as I was, and, to my surprise, I came face to face with – Angela!

At first I thought Angela was playing a trick on me. "Why didn't you tell me you were coming?" I asked. [3]_____

"I'm sorry, do I know you?" she asked, rather suspiciously.
"Come on, Angela!" I said. "What's going on?"
[4]_____ "I don't believe it!" she exclaimed. "People often confuse me with my sister at home, but it's never happened here in Egypt before! Hi, I'm Caroline."

Before I left Cairo, I got together with Caroline a few more times. <u>As soon as</u> I got home, I called Angela. "You told me you had a sister, but you forgot to mention that you were identical twins!" I said.

But still, meeting Caroline in that crowded tourist spot was incredible. [5]_____

1 Read the blog post quickly, ignoring the blanks. Choose the best summary.

a The narrator went to Egypt, but didn't enjoy his vacation.

b The narrator went to Egypt and met his friend Angela there.

c The narrator went on vacation to Egypt and met his friend's sister by chance.

2 Read the blog post again. Match blanks 1–5 with sentences a–g. There are two extra sentences.

a It was a chance in a million!

b The sun was high in the clear, blue sky.

c I was so excited to be there at last, looking at these incredible structures.

d Then the woman started laughing.

e She had fair, wavy hair and was wearing a large sun hat.

f But she just gave me a strange look.

g That reminded me of my old dream.

3 Look at the <u>underlined</u> words *as soon as*, *before*, *after*, and *until* in the text. Use each word or phrase twice to complete these sentences.

1 Carlos will need to borrow some money _____ he can buy a car.

2 _____ I met James, I knew I would marry him.

3 I spoke to Laurence _____ the show, and he said he had enjoyed it.

4 Dougal hopes to work as an engineer _____ college.

5 I'm not hungry, thank you. We ate _____ we went out.

6 Keir took his exams in June, but he won't get the results _____ August.

7 Please let me know _____ you have any news about Paul.

8 Priti had to stay in the office _____ she had finished all her work.

4 Write a blog post about an amazing event. Include two of these sentences in your blog.

• It was an amazing coincidence!

• He was tall with long, blond hair and blue eyes.

• I felt very sad when it was time for us to say goodbye.

• It was one of the happiest days of my life.

• Unfortunately, we had missed the last train.

• It hadn't stopped raining since we arrived.

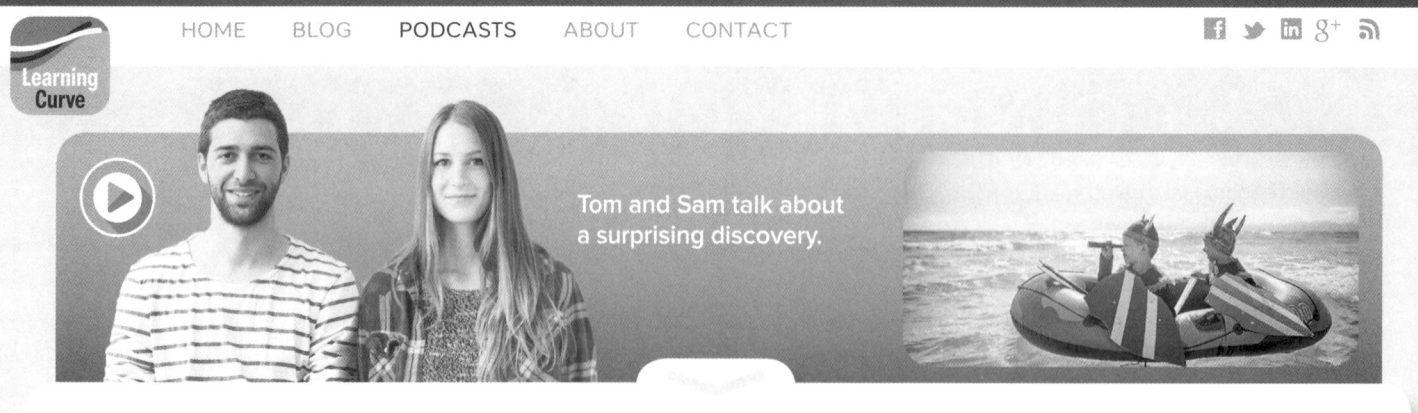

HOME   BLOG   PODCASTS   ABOUT   CONTACT

Learning Curve

Tom and Sam talk about a surprising discovery.

LISTENING

1 ▶ 2.5 Listen to the podcast and choose the best summary of the story.

The man told Tom

a how he had met his wife.

b how he had found his wife in an old photo from when he was a child.

c that he and his wife used to go to the same place on vacation when they were children.

2 ▶ 2.5 Listen again and choose the correct options to complete the sentences.

1 Sam and Tom are wearing similar shoes, but Tom's are
   a made by a different company.
   b much bigger.
   c a different color.

2 The guests on today's show are all describing
   a very surprising things that have happened to them.
   b stories about old photographs.
   c an early get-together with a person who became his or her partner.

3 Adam and Natalie got married
   a while they were in college.
   b a few years after college.
   c just after finishing college.

4 Adam and Natalie discovered that they had
   a been to the same place on vacation.
   b both been to the same school.
   c both been to Mexico.

5 All of the photographs that Adam's mother had brought were
   a from their vacation in California.
   b from their vacations in Mexico.
   c ones in which Adam appeared.

6 Adam was amazed because
   a his brother was in the photograph.
   b he and his brother were on the beach in the photograph.
   c Natalie was in the photograph, too.

READING

1 Read Tom's blog on page 13 and and choose the best summary.

a the different places where Tom has seen celebrities in London

b how easy it is to see celebrities in London

c the experience of seeing a celebrity for the first time

2 Write T for true sentences, F for false sentences, and DS when the writer doesn't say.

1 Tom saw the famous musician in the morning. ....

2 He was late for work when he saw the musician. ....

3 The people near Tom also noticed the musician. ....

4 Tom and the musician spoke to each other. ....

5 This was the first celebrity that Tom had seen. ....

6 Tom's friend is a big fan of James Bond movies. ....

7 Tom thinks that his readers might not believe what his friend told Tom. ....

8 Tom shares his roommate's interest in celebrity vloggers. ....

9 Tom hopes he'll see more celebrities in the future. ....

3 Find six examples of *-ed/-ing* adjectives in the text.

HOME **BLOG** PODCASTS ABOUT CONTACT

Tom writes about seeing someone famous.

CELEBRITY SPOTTING

Well, that was an exciting way to start the day! There I was at Baker Street station, on my way to work. I was going down the escalator toward the trains when suddenly I saw Adele on the other escalator. She was going up toward the exit. Yes, it really was Adele, the pop star with one of the biggest-selling albums of all time! I was absolutely amazed. If you've had the experience of suddenly seeing a face that you've only ever seen before at the movies or on an album cover you'll know how astonishing this experience is. You can't believe your eyes – you don't think it's really happening. Am I dreaming? What's going on?

Anyway, judging by the excited reaction of the people around me (*Adele, wow! It's Adele! Oh my gosh! I don't believe it!* etc.) I can tell you with absolute certainty that it really was Adele, the singer. And, at last, I was able to proudly tell my friends and family that I'd finally met a famous person. (OK, I didn't exactly meet her…) They say that in London you're never more than a few meters away from a celebrity, but before this morning (and after six whole years in this city), I hadn't laid eyes on a single actor or musician. Very disappointing – oh, wait a minute, I once saw the depressed shopkeeper from a daytime soap opera. Does that count? It does? OK, I'd seen exactly one actor in my six years here! And I can't even remember his name!

Meanwhile, my friend Claire, who lives in a tiny little village outside Oxford, seems to see a famous actor most weeks. For example, if I remember correctly, in the last ten years, she's spotted no less than *three* James Bonds, past and present, in and around Oxford. (As I write that, I realize that you might think that my friend has a rather vivid imagination.) And my roommate here in London sees a celebrity most weeks. Though, when I say "celebrity," of course, we all have different ideas about what a celebrity is. Those of you who know my roommate are aware that he is a *very* enthusiastic follower of five or six "celebrity vloggers." Now, I don't even know the names of these "celebrities" and I'm pretty sure that I could walk past *any* of them in the street without recognizing them.

Still, now I've spotted one of the biggest celebrities on the planet – perhaps she'll be the first of many?

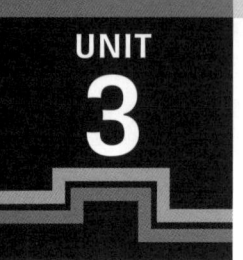

UNIT 3 People

3A LANGUAGE

GRAMMAR: Future forms: present continuous, *be going to* and *will*

1 Choose the correct verbs to complete the sentences.

1 "Do you know Rocco's date of birth?" "No, *I'll ask / I'm asking* him later."

2 It's a beautiful day. *Will we go / Should we go* to the beach?

3 What *will you do / are you doing* next weekend?

4 I failed my driving test. *Are you helping / Will you help* me practice?

5 *Are we going to / Will we* invite Sara to their wedding?

6 "I can't do my homework." "*I'm helping / I'll help* you, if you'd like."

7 Max *will come / is coming* back from Australia on Friday.

8 I'm going to a concert tomorrow. *Should I / Am I going to* get you a ticket?

2 Complete the conversations with the present continuous, *going to*, *will*, or *should* and the verb in parentheses. There may be more than one answer.

A ¹_____ (visit) anywhere exciting on vacation this year?

B Yes, Kenya. But we ²_____ (not travel) with a group.

A I've got a fantastic book about Kenya. I ³_____ (lend) it to you.

A The movie you were talking about is on next week. ⁴_____ (go) and see it together?

B Great! I ⁵_____ (get) tickets later.

A Really? I work closer to the theater than you.

B Don't worry – I ⁶_____ (do) it online.

A ⁷_____ (make) dinner for you tonight?

B Actually, I ⁸_____ (meet) Joe this evening. We ⁹_____ (play) tennis and then get pizza.

A OK, I ¹⁰_____ (not make) anything for you, then.

VOCABULARY: Personality adjectives

3 Read the sentences and match the people with the adjectives in the box. There are two extra adjectives.

> unsociable   dishonest   insensitive   impolite
> easygoing   disorganized   confident   impatient

1 Robert would be very happy to make a speech in front of 1,000 people. _____

2 Kira knows I don't have much money, but she keeps telling me about expensive things she's bought. _____

3 Andrew's always missing meetings because he doesn't write them in his diary. _____

4 On the weekends, Adam's usually happy to do whatever his friends suggest. _____

5 Gloria doesn't like parties – she'd rather stay at home and read a book. _____

6 Chuck hates having to wait for other people – he just wants to get moving with things. _____

4 Complete the personality adjectives.

1 Why did you refuse to speak to Suzie? That was really u_____.

2 Maya has been very h_____ – she's cleaned the bathroom and prepared dinner.

3 Don't ask Helen for a ride if you need to be there on time – she's too u_____.

4 Laurie is feeling a_____ about his exam because he hasn't prepared well enough.

5 Ella always makes the decisions in our house – she's extremely s_____.

6 It's d_____ to tell the customers that the milk is organic when it's not.

7 It was so i_____ of them to talk while the professor was speaking.

8 Everyone at my new school is very f_____, so I didn't feel at all lonely.

PRONUNCIATION: *going to*

5 ▶ 3.1 Check (✔) the sentences where *going to* can be pronounced /ˈɡʌnə/. Listen and check.

1 Are you going to buy Hamish a present? _____

2 Alice is going to Cleveland next week. _____

3 I think my mom's going to be really angry. _____

4 I'm going to ask my teacher to explain. _____

5 Is Tom going to the concert with you? _____

6 Are we going to have dinner now? _____

READING: Reading for specific information

Twin personalities?

A Mark and Ollie are identical twins. They look so alike that when they were little even their mother had to look carefully to see which one she was speaking to, and they certainly used this to play tricks on teachers or friends! Now they are twenty, and although they still look very similar (Mark is slightly larger as he works out at the gym most days), their personalities could hardly be more different.

B "I'm the sociable one," Mark says. "I love meeting new people, trying new activities, traveling, things like that. Ollie's the opposite – it's not that he's unfriendly, but he'd rather stay at home and read a book."

C So how common is it for twins to have such different personalities? Well, psychologists used to think that twins developed pretty much independently, each one shaped by his or her own life experiences. So they would have thought that Mark and Ollie were typical. However, recent research has challenged this view.

D Researchers from Edinburgh University studied 800 sets of twins. Focusing on qualities that contribute to success in life (such as self-control and willingness to work hard), they found that twins are twice as likely to share personality traits than other brothers and sisters. Amazingly, a similar study carried out at the University of Minnesota found that twins raised in different families are even more likely to share personality traits. In fact, two subjects of the study, brothers Jim Lewis and Jim Springer, who were brought up separately, were so similar that it was almost impossible to tell them apart.

E Twins Rachel and Annie, who grew up together, aren't surprised that twins raised in the same family end up being more different from each other. "Since we looked so alike, people sometimes treated us as if we were just one person," Annie explains. "And we hated it. That's why we made a deliberate effort to be different. When Rachel started playing soccer, I took up the piano, so she became the athletic one, and I was the creative one."

1 Skim the text quickly. Match paragraphs A–E with summaries 1–5.

1 Ideas about twins and personality have changed over time. _____

2 These two brothers look very similar. _____

3 Research shows that twins naturally have similar personalities. _____

4 Why two sisters want to be different from one another. _____

5 How one man differs from his brother. _____

2 Read the questions and <u>underline</u> the key words. Then choose the correct answers.

1 What could Mark and Ollie do because they looked so similar?
a make people believe that one of them was the other
b miss school
c make their friends laugh

2 How different are Mark and Ollie's personalities?
a very different
b slightly different
c not very different

3 In the past, where did scientists believe most personality traits in twins came from?
a the personality of their parents
b things that happened in their lives
c the way their families treated them

4 What areas of personality did the Edinburgh research study most?
a all aspects
b aspects that are likely to be different between twins
c aspects connected to people's achievements

5 Why did Rachel and Annie deliberately try to be different from each other?
a They didn't want other people to know who each girl was.
b It was important for them to have their own identities.
c They thought it would be boring for them to be the same.

3 Choose the correct words to complete the sentences.

1 The bus broke down. *So / Since / That's why* we're so late.

2 I didn't invite Polly *so / as / that's why* she's not one of my friends.

3 Alex has lost his key, *so / since / that's why* he'll have to break the window to get in.

4 Let's have a cup of tea *since / so / that's why* we're still waiting for Clara to arrive.

5 I know Bella pretty well *that's why / so / as* we work in the same building.

6 Ruth didn't have a towel, *since / so / that's why* she dried herself on an old T-shirt.

GRAMMAR: Defining and non-defining relative clauses

1 Choose the correct options. Parentheses show that you can omit the pronoun.

1 Gary walked to the station, _____ his friend was waiting.
   a who **b** that **c** where **d** (which)

2 The box, _____ was very heavy, contained more than twenty books.
   a (which) **b** which **c** (that) **d** who

3 He's the man _____ lives in the house across the street.
   a whose **b** (who) **c** which **d** that

4 Is this the car _____ you're thinking of buying?
   a (that) **b** where **c** whose **d** (who)

5 Lucas, _____ parents are in the army, has moved many times.
   a who **b** (that) **c** whose **d** which

6 There will be a prize for the person _____ writes the best story.
   a (who) **b** (that) **c** whose **d** who

7 She's the woman _____ works in the bank.
   a (who) **b** that **c** where **d** (that)

8 Did I show you the photo _____ I took?
   a (that) **b** whose **c** which **d** where

2 Write relative clauses to include the information in parentheses. Add commas where necessary and omit the relative pronouns where possible.

1 Where have you put the bag? (I gave it to you.)
   Where have you put the bag I gave you?

2 My aunt is planning to sail around the world. (She's very adventurous.)
   My aunt _____
   is planning to sail around the world.

3 The woman is very upset. (Her dog has run away.)
   The woman _____
   is very upset.

4 I've been to the office. (Rupert works there.)
   I've been to the office
   _____ works.

5 There's the man. (He comes to cut the grass.)
   There's the man
   _____

6 I'm going to New York! (It's exciting.)
   I'm going to New York
   _____ exciting!

7 Is that the boy? (You told me about him.)
   Is that the boy
   _____ about?

VOCABULARY: Relationships

3 Read the sentences and check (✔) True or False.

		True	False
1	Close friends always live near each other.	True	False
2	Children in the U.S. usually live with their relatives.	True	False
3	It's upsetting to have a falling out with a friend.	True	False
4	Most people would like to get along well with their family.	True	False
5	You can't have classmates if you're not a student.	True	False
6	If people make up, they can never be friends again.	True	False
7	We introduce someone to people they've met before.	True	False
8	Your next-door neighbor lives in the nearest house.	True	False
9	Any two friends can be described as "a couple."	True	False
10	If you have a lot in common with someone, lots of things about your lives are similar.	True	False

4 Complete the text with relationship words.

I moved to Mexico City two years ago to start a new job. At work, my new ¹c_____ were very friendly, but I was still lonely at first. Back at home in Tijuana, I used to hang out with my ²b_____ friend Alejandro most weekends, and I missed him a lot. However, things soon got better. I joined a gym, and I gradually got to ³k_____ people. Now I ⁴g_____ along especially well with a guy called Felipe. In fact, it was Felipe who ⁵i_____ me to my ⁶g_____, Mercedes – we're getting married next year. Mercedes and I have so much in ⁷c_____ – we are both engineers, and we love music. We also have very strong opinions, and we sometimes ⁸a_____ – especially about politics – but we always ⁹m_____ up before too long! Last year, I took Mercedes to Tijuana to meet my ¹⁰p_____ and some of my other ¹¹r_____. They loved her. While we were there, we got ¹²t_____ with all my old friends, too, which was great!

PRONUNCIATION: Pausing in relative clauses

5 ▶3.2 Read the sentences aloud, pausing when there are commas. Listen, check, and repeat.

1 We often eat paella, which is a Spanish dish.

2 Is that the man who lives next door to Sam?

3 My colleagues, who are really friendly, planned a birthday party for me.

4 I get along well with my brother, who is two years older than me.

5 The town where I grew up is very small.

6 This necklace, which belonged to my grandmother, is my favorite.

SPEAKING: Giving and responding to news

1 ▶ 3.3 Listen to the conversation between Lily and her roommate, Anne. Are the following statements true (T) or false (F)?

1 Lily is pleased that Raj is coming. _____
2 Raj called when Lily was not at home. _____
3 Raj forgot to apply for a visa. _____
4 Raj has only been to the UK once before. _____
5 In the end, Raj is allowed to travel to the UK. _____
6 Anne does not want her to become too friendly with Raj. _____

2 ▶ 3.3 Listen again and choose the correct options.

1 How did Anne give Lily some bad news?
 a I'm sorry, but I have something bad to tell you.
 b I'm afraid I have some bad news.
 c I'm really sorry to give you this bad news.

2 How did Lily respond?
 a Oh no, I don't believe it!
 b Oh, that's horrible!
 c Oh no, that's terrible!

3 How did Anne show sympathy?
 a That's terrible!
 b What a shame!
 c It's not fair!

4 How did Anne give Lily some good news?
 a Guess what?
 b Great news!
 c I have some good news for you.

5 How did Lily respond?
 a I'm so happy!
 b That's fantastic news!
 c Oh, that's a relief!

6 How did Anne show that she was pleased, too?
 a I'm so happy for you!
 b I'm absolutely thrilled for you!
 c That's fantastic news!

3 ▶ 3.4 Complete the conversations. Then listen and check.

1 **A** I have some good n_____! I passed my driving test!
 B C_____! Now you can give me a ride to school!

2 **A** I'm really s_____ to give you this news, but I can't come to your wedding. I have an important exam that day.
 B Oh, what a s_____! I really wanted you to be there.

3 **A** Great n_____! The doctor says there's nothing wrong with me.
 B Oh, that's a r_____!

4 **A** A_____ what? I just got an e-mail saying I've won a major poetry competition.
 B Oh, wow! I'm absolutely t_____ for you!

5 **A** I'm a_____ I have some bad news. Toby's dog has died.
 B Oh no, that's t_____!

4 Mr. Allsworth (A) is telling his student Cara (B) that her grades aren't good enough to get accepted into a program where she had hoped to study. Read the conversation and complete A with your own words.

A (Say that you have some bad news for her.)
_____

B Oh no, what is it?

A (Explain that she needs at least a grade B to get accepted into the program.)
_____

B Yes, that's right. If I get less than a grade B, they won't accept me.

A (Give her the bad news.)
_____

B Oh no! That means I'll have to take the exam again.

A (Tell her that you're really sorry.)
_____

B Thank you. I guess I'll need to work harder next time.

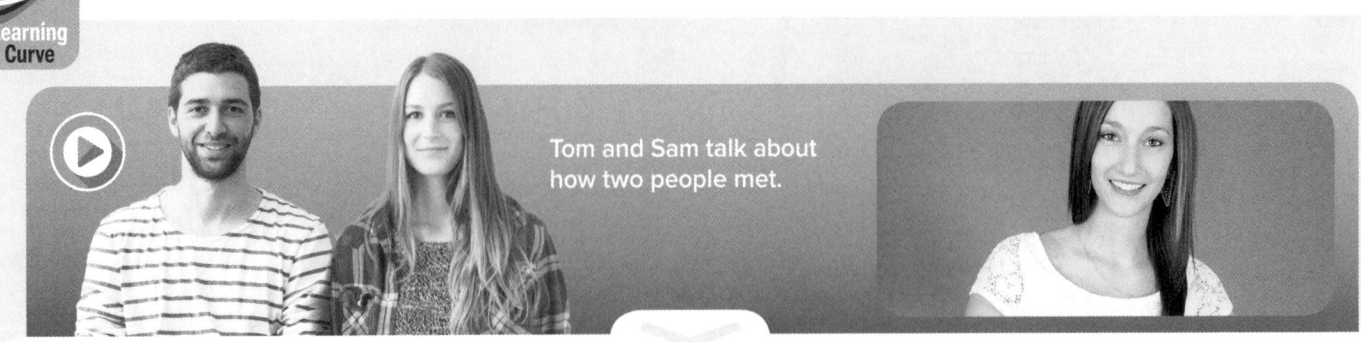

Learning Curve

Tom and Sam talk about how two people met.

LISTENING

1 ▶ **3.5** Listen to the podcast and number words a–f in the order you hear them (1–6).

  a bathroom   _____

  b cell phone number   _____

  c party   _____

  d vacation   _____

  e cloth   _____

  f drink   _____

2 ▶ **3.5** Listen again and complete the sentences with one or two words.

  1 Daisy and Izzie are now _____.

  2 One of Izzie's _____ introduced them at a party.

  3 Julia thought they would have a lot _____.

  4 Izzie thought that Daisy was _____, but now understands that she is just shy.

  5 Daisy thought that Izzie was _____ and _____.

  6 Izzie ran off to _____ to find a cloth, but Daisy had disappeared.

  7 Daisy went to hide in the bathroom because she felt _____.

  8 Izzie didn't realize that Daisy was so _____ because of the accident with Izzie's drink.

  9 When they got together again after the party, Daisy _____ to Izzie.

  10 Next week, they are traveling to _____ together.

READING

1 Read Sam's blog on page 19 and number points a–e in the order they appear (1–5).

  a Best friends who are different are more likely to help each other.   _____

  b Best friends find the differences between them interesting.   _____

  c Friendships are more likely to succeed between people who are very different.   _____

  d We don't try to be better than friends who are very different from us.   _____

  e With "opposite friends" we are prepared to try out things we haven't done before.   _____

2 Check (✓) the statements that are true.

  1 Sam has always had a very strong opinion about this subject.   _____

  2 The researchers did not study many pairs of friends.   _____

  3 Romantic relationships generally work better between personalities that are similar.   _____

  4 Sam is good at finding her way to places.   _____

  5 There are advantages when one friend provides a skill that the other friend does not have.   _____

  6 Friends who are similar to us encourage us to try new things.   _____

  7 Friends who have different qualities from each other are less competitive.   _____

  8 The perfect friend would be someone who behaves in exactly the same way as you.   _____

HOME **BLOG** PODCASTS ABOUT CONTACT

Sam writes about what attracts us to other people.

OPPOSITES | ATTRACT!

Have you ever found yourself saying, "Opposites attract!" about a couple that you know, or a friendship in your social circle? I know I have. (I've never been able to decide whether it was true, by the way!) I just read a fascinating article on the subject, and I'm going to share the main points with you. (A bit of background for your information: researchers studied the personalities of over a thousand pairs of best friends.)

So, it turns out we were right about friends. Friendships do work best between people with very different qualities where, for example, best friend A is confident, disorganized, and easygoing, and best friend B is shy, reliable, and anxious. (Interestingly, this is not the case for romantic relationships, where previous studies have shown that opposite personality types are *less likely* to lead to successful, long-term relationships.) There are several reasons for this.

1 The "opposites attract" friends bring different qualities and abilities to the relationship, and this is useful. For example, the person with no sense of direction (that's me!) will probably have a better time when he or she is with a friend who knows exactly how to get to where they're going. The very shy person (er, not me!) will have more success at a party with a sociable friend who can introduce him or her to new people, and so on.

2 Opposites force each other out of their comfort zones. You know how it goes – you feel anxious about doing something new for the first time, but, afterwards, you're really glad that your friend persuaded you to do it. Friends who have the same interests and qualities as us don't challenge us to experience new things. Friends who are very different from us introduce us to new activities and experiences and this, apparently, helps us to "grow" as people.

3 Opposites are free to be themselves. With their different strengths and skills, they're not both trying to be "the organized one," for example, or "the sociable one." Neither friend is competing in the relationship. This results in a happier, less competitive friendship.

4 Opposites don't get bored with each other. Simply, the differences between us keep us interested. This point reminds me that I once read somewhere that it would be people's worst nightmare if they met themselves. (Imagine knowing exactly what the other "you" was thinking and how this other "you" was going to respond to something …)

The next time I find myself getting frustrated because I don't understand why a friend is behaving in a particular way, I'm going to stop and celebrate the differences between us.

Places and homes

GRAMMAR: Quantifiers

1 Choose the correct options to complete the sentences.

1 This soup is horrible! I put _____ salt in it.
   a too much   **b** plenty of   **c** too many

2 The local people gave us _____ of their traditional food.
   a few   **b** a little   **c** much

3 We couldn't buy clothes because we had _____ money.
   a not any   **b** not enough   **c** no

4 There wasn't _____ room for us all to get on the bus.
   a lots of   **b** enough   **c** plenty

5 There's _____ chance that Hal will win the competition.
   a not much   **b** not enough   **c** too much

6 You can't swim today. It's _____ cold!
   a too much   **b** enough   **c** too

7 _____ people want ice cream in the winter.
   a Little   **b** Not much   **c** Not many

8 We couldn't make a fire because there wasn't _____ wood.
   a plenty   **b** any   **c** lots of

2 Read the sentences and write appropriate responses. Use the words in parentheses in the correct form.

1 The bus holds 40 people, and 80 people want to travel.
   The bus _____ .
   (is/big)

2 You can bring your whole family to stay.
   We _____
   (plenty/bedrooms)

3 I can't afford to buy this coat.
   It _____
   (too/money)

4 It's hard to buy nice clothes where I live.
   There _____
   in town. (many/stores)

5 The museum is really popular with tourists.
   _____ to visit it. (people/want)

6 Dinner's not ready yet.
   You will have to _____
   (wait/minutes)

7 We can't have omelets for lunch.
   There _____
   (no/eggs)

VOCABULARY: Compound nouns

3 Match the two parts of the sentences.

1 You shouldn't ride your bike _____
2 I bought a pair of pants and some plates _____
3 Harry was late getting home because he was stuck _____
4 Sue drove into town and left her car _____
5 There is a good collection of modern paintings _____
6 We usually play squash on the courts _____

   a in a traffic jam.
   b at the sports center.
   c in a pedestrian area.
   d in a parking lot.
   e at a department store.
   f at the art gallery.

4 Complete the text with compound nouns.

I live just outside the city, but my office is downtown, so I have to commute to work every day. When the weather's good, I ride my bike. Luckily, there is a good ¹_____ path that goes almost all the way to my office. And when it rains, there's an excellent ²_____ transportation system, so I never use my car to get to work – it would be silly to spend time sitting in a traffic ³_____ when there's a bus every ten minutes! This is a great city for a young person like me to live in. There's a huge ⁴_____ mall – I often go to the sporting-goods stores there on my lunch hour. And the night ⁵_____ is great, too, with plenty of movie theaters, restaurants, and ⁶_____ clubs. There's a big sports ⁷_____ near my apartment, where I play soccer with my friends on the weekends.

PRONUNCIATION: Sentence stress

5 ▶4.1 Read the sentences and <u>underline</u> the syllables you think will be stressed. Listen and check.

1 The children made lots of noise.
2 Are there enough sandwiches?
3 We don't have any towels.
4 She gave me too much rice.
5 Make sure there's plenty of water.
6 Let's pick a few strawberries.

LISTENING: Understanding key points

1 ▶4.2 Patrizia has gone to see a real estate agent in order to rent an apartment. Listen to their conversation and choose the correct options.

1 Why does Patrizia want to live alone?
   a She is worried that other people won't like her dog.
   b She has had her own place for a long time and does not want to share again.
   c She thinks it's cheaper to live on your own.

2 Why will it be more difficult for her to find an apartment?
   a There aren't many apartments where you can keep a dog.
   b There aren't many luxury apartments available.
   c A lot of apartments are not clean and bright.

3 She says that it's not important to live close to school because
   a having somewhere for her dog is more important.
   b she is willing to travel a pretty long way by bike.
   c she is only going there for one year.

4 Why does she want to live somewhere with lots of restaurants and cafés?
   a She will not have time to cook.
   b Areas like that are more interesting.
   c She doesn't want to cook her own meals.

5 She doesn't want the first apartment the real estate agent suggests because
   a she hates riding in elevators.
   b she doesn't want to live with people who work downtown.
   c she doesn't think she would like the area.

6 Why is the second apartment more suitable for her dog?
   a They will not need to ride in an elevator.
   b The dog likes walking up and down the stairs.
   c It is in a lively area.

2 ▶4.3 Listen to the sentences from Patrizia's conversation. Focus on the way they use different words to repeat key points. Complete the sentences.

1 Did you want a place of your own, or are you happy to _____ with other people?.

2 No, I've lived _____ for four years now, and I don't want to live with other people again.

3 Obviously, an apartment just for you will be a little more expensive. It's _____ to share.

4 It's not very interesting around there, is it? I'm worried it could be a bit _____.

5 It's in a much livelier area. I think it would be more _____.

3 ▶4.4 Look at the sentences. Use the mark _ to show links between consonants with similar sounds. One sentence has more than one link. Listen, check, and repeat.

1 When do you plan to leave Venice?

2 I have to take Katie to the station.

3 Dan's mom made him stay inside.

4 Polly told me she'd done yoga before.

5 Where did you buy your jacket?

6 I tried to fix Sue's broken laptop.

7 I hope Lara won't feel lonely.

8 Morgan made a really good dessert.

4 Use a different form of the same verb to complete both sentences in 1–8.

1 a I have _____ Kelly for a long time.
   b We will contact you when we _____ more facts about the situation.

2 a We _____ a great time in France last summer.
   b Why don't you _____ something to eat before we set off again?

3 a Unfortunately, Simon's team _____ the game.
   b I gave Mel my address and phone number so that we don't _____ contact.

4 a When I _____ Eva for the first time, I thought she was really scary!
   b Izzie's planning to _____ a friend for coffee this afternoon.

5 a I feel terrible – I think I've _____ Toni's cold.
   b Amit _____ a cab when he misses the last bus.

6 a My sister _____ borrowing my clothes without asking.
   b George said he would come back, and he _____ his promise.

7 a Suzi was late because she _____ her bus.
   b I'm sure you would _____ your brother if he went to live abroad.

8 a Is it OK to _____ photos in here?
   b The man came into the room and _____ his coat off.

GRAMMAR: Comparatives and superlatives, *as … as*

1 Complete the sentences with the phrases in the box.

> the best of   as good as   less difficult
> the most difficult   by far the best
> the least difficult   one of the best
> as difficult as

1 Louis is _____ soccer player on our team.

2 Clara was _____ pianists I had ever heard.

3 Saying goodbye to my parents was _____ thing I've ever done.

4 After I gave up sugar, losing weight wasn't _____ I thought it would be.

5 Kari is really stressed out. She needs to find a _____ job.

6 Pilar, Rafaelle, and Maya are all good at math, but Maya is _____ the three.

7 Neil's new, so we're giving him _____ work to begin with.

8 I don't think this restaurant is _____ it used to be.

2 Complete the sentences with the adjectives in the box. Add any other words necessary.

> hot   bad   angry   expensive   easy
> late   far   beautiful

1 I failed my French exam but I passed Spanish. I find Spanish far _____ French.

2 It takes me ten minutes to bike home, but it takes Aidan 20 minutes because he lives _____ away than me.

3 We stay inside around lunchtime because it is _____ part of the day.

4 I didn't stay up _____ as my friends because I had to get up early.

5 The Taj Mahal is _____ building I have ever seen.

6 When we tried to apologize, Sara seemed to get even _____.

7 We had very little money, so we bought _____ computer in the store.

8 I thought his last novel was bad, but this one is even _____ than that.

VOCABULARY: Describing homes

3 Choose the correct words to complete the sentences.

1 Sophia has three sofas in her *basic / spacious / cozy* living room.

2 Tom's kitchen is really *old-fashioned / stylish / modern* – he certainly doesn't have a dishwasher!

3 It's a two-minute walk to the supermarket, so that's very *comfortable / convenient / basic*.

4 They have a *bright / convenient / huge* garden that takes up a lot of their time.

5 There's a shower but no bathtub because my bathroom is so *tiny / cozy / old-fashioned*.

6 This room will look more *basic / spacious / cozy* with some rugs.

7 Lou's bedroom only has a closet and a bed, so it's pretty *basic / stylish / bright*.

8 Her kitchen's *stylish / dark / cozy* with that big tree outside.

4 Complete the words.

1 My apartment's on the _____p floor and has a great view.

2 Furniture we didn't use was stored down in the b_____t.

3 I live in the s_____s because it's cheaper than downtown.

4 There is just one shopping m_____ in the small town where I live.

5 Grandma has a f_____ floor apartment without stairs.

6 Does this t_____n have a library and a post office?

7 My bedroom has a b_____y outside that I often sit on.

8 In the summer, do you often eat out on the roof t_____e?

9 Max lives on the sixteenth floor of an a_____t building.

10 They had been to the c_____y, walking among the trees and fields.

PRONUNCIATION: /ə/ sound

5 ▶4.5 Listen to the sentences. Do the underlined words contain the /ə/ sound? Write ✓ or ✗.

1 My sister's <u>not</u> <u>as</u> tall <u>as</u> me.   _____ _____ _____

2 Dan is by <u>far</u> <u>the</u> best tennis player I <u>know</u>.   _____ _____ _____

3 It's <u>a</u> bit <u>cooler</u> today <u>than</u> yesterday.   _____ _____ _____

4 Gabi is <u>better</u> <u>than</u> me at <u>ballet</u>.   _____ _____ _____

5 I'd like to get <u>a</u> <u>bigger</u> <u>apartment</u>.   _____ _____ _____

6 This is the <u>longest</u> <u>of</u> all <u>the</u> books.   _____ _____ _____

WRITING: Writing an informal e-mail

1 Read Owen's e-mail to his friend Gabe. Divide it into six paragraphs by putting a / at the end of each one.

Hey Gabe,

Great to hear from you! Sorry for not writing sooner. Fantastic news about your new job in Los Angeles! I hope you're enjoying it. I hear the nightlife is really good there. Can't wait to come and see you. Do you have your own apartment? Anyway, everything's fine here, except that my sister was in a car crash last week! Luckily, nobody was hurt, but the car's in terrible shape. It's going to cost her a fortune to repair it. So she's riding her bike everywhere at the moment and complaining about it all the time! Speaking of bike riding, did I tell you that Kenny and I are planning to take our bikes to Colorado this summer? There's a great route through the mountains that we want to try. Not sure if Kenny can ride up a mountain, though. ;-) He hasn't trained much recently because he has a new girlfriend, and he's spending all of his time with her. You could come with us, too, if you're free – you're in much better shape than Kenny, after all! By the way, did you hear that the Los Angeles Angels aren't doing too well this year? Not sure if I'll buy a season ticket next year. It's hard to support a team that loses. Anyway, have to go now – need to be at work early tomorrow, so it has to be an early night. Let me know what you think about the Colorado trip.

All the best,

Owen

2 Find the informal sentences in the e-mail that have the same meaning as these more formal sentences (1–6).

1 I am looking forward to visiting you in Los Angeles.
2 I should stop writing now.
3 I apologize for not replying to your e-mail before now.
4 I was very pleased to hear that you have a new job.
5 I have not decided if I should buy a season ticket next year.
6 Thank you very much for your e-mail.

3 Read the pairs of sentences (1–6). Fill in the blanks with the discourse markers in the box. There may be more than one answer.

So, …   Anyway, …   By the way, …   Speaking of …

1 … and he's going to be in the hospital for about a month.
_____ I also have some much happier news to give you – I got the job at the restaurant!
2 … I've worked a lot of extra hours recently, so I've had a bit more money, and I've bought myself a really good tent.
_____ camping, do you feel like taking a trip next weekend?
3 … so it's really important that you sign the document.
_____ have you seen Martha recently? I heard that she broke up with Josh.

4 … and I ended up missing my plane – it was such a disaster!
_____ Matt says to tell you that he wants his coat back. He says you borrowed it a month ago.
5 … and we all went out to celebrate because Hayley passed her driving test.
_____ driving tests, when are you taking yours?
6 … I had to borrow a bike from George to get there on time!
_____ what do you think of George's new girlfriend?

4 Imagine you are Gabe. Reply to Owen's e-mail. Write six paragraphs and include some of the informal discourse markers from exercise 3. Use some of these ideas.

• Express sympathy for Owen's sister.
• Talk about your new job and apartment in Los Angeles.
• Invite Owen to stay.
• Accept Owen's invitation to go bicycling in Colorado OR give a reason why you can't go.
• Say something about the Los Angeles Angels or a team you support.

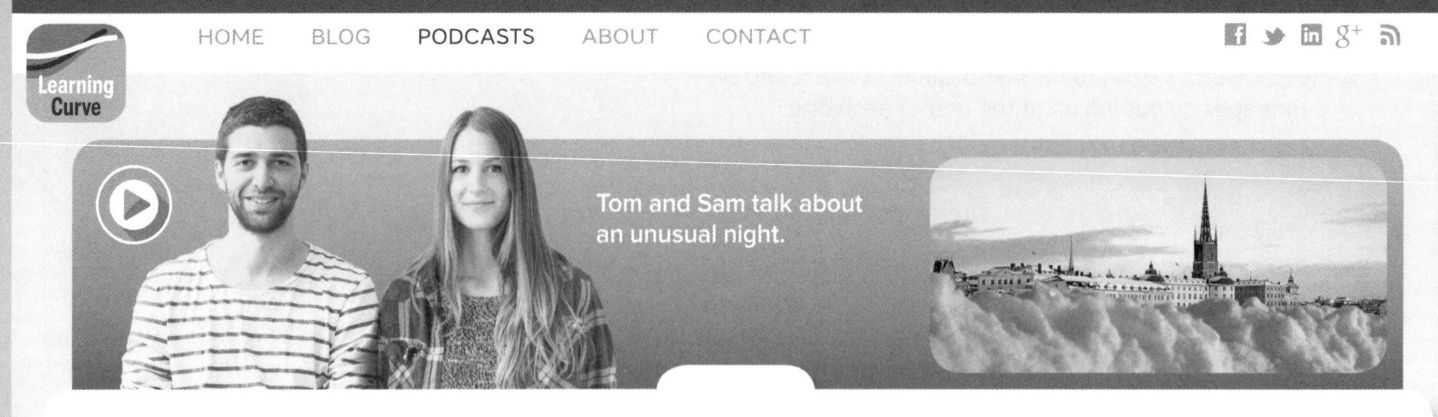

HOME   BLOG   **PODCASTS**   ABOUT   CONTACT

Tom and Sam talk about an unusual night.

LISTENING

1 ▶ 4.6 Listen to the podcast and number a–e in the order in which they happen (1–5).

a Olivia and her daughter got into a cab. ....

b Olivia and her daughter were shopping in a department store. ....

c They found themselves in a terrible traffic jam. ....

d They slept in the department store. ....

e They returned to the department store. ....

2 ▶ 4.6 Listen again and choose the correct options.

1 According to Tom, Sam always sleeps
   a in unusual places.
   b in expensive hotels.
   c on friends' sofas.

2 What caused the problem for Olivia and her daughter?
   a There was heavy snow.
   b There weren't enough cabs.
   c The store closed early.

3 After getting out of the cab, where did they go to?
   a a nearby café
   b a bedding store
   c the same department store

4 While they were waiting for the snow to stop, they
   a looked out of the window.
   b sat on the beds.
   c ate some food.

5 Where did they spend the night?
   a in the basement
   b on the first floor
   c on the second floor

6 How was Olivia and her daughter's night at the department store?
   a rather uncomfortable
   b very comfortable
   c pretty cold

READING

1 Read Simon's blog on page 25 and choose the best summary of Simon's reasons for visiting his friend, Al.

a He wanted to show his friends that he could do new things.

b He wanted to help Al build a hut to sleep in.

c He wanted to find out what it was like to live in the country.

2 According to the blog post, are the sentences true (T), false (F), or the writer doesn't say (DS)?

1 Simon loves cities, but hasn't always lived in one. ....

2 Simon enjoys the nightlife that the city has to offer. ....

3 Simon often uses public transportation where he lives. ....

4 Simon isn't always completely satisfied with city life. ....

5 Al prefers cold showers to hot showers. ....

6 Simon didn't leave Al's field all week. ....

7 Simon did all the cooking while he was staying with Al. ....

8 While Simon was staying with him, Al slept outdoors. ....

3 Find compound nouns in the text to match definitions 1–6.

1 A place where you can get exercise

2 A place where you can buy lots of different things

3 A system of vehicles that anyone can use

4 When cars and other vehicles are in a line and cannot move

5 A place where you can see paintings

6 A place where you go dancing

Guest blogger Simon writes about his visit to the country.

GETTING AWAY FROM IT ALL

As readers of this blog know, at heart I'm a city person, despite growing up on a farm. OK, there are plenty of things about the city that I don't particularly like. For example, you won't find me in a nightclub at three o'clock in the morning, and, as I've said before, I'm no fan of this city's many shopping malls. However, there are certain aspects of city life that I really do appreciate – the art galleries, the theaters, the restaurants and cafés, and so on. And as a non-driver, I find the public transportation you get in a city very convenient.

That said, from time to time I wonder whether there's a better life out there in the country, away from all the traffic jams, the constant noise, and, of course, the pollution. (Doesn't everyone?) So to explore this idea, last week I went to stay with my old high school friend, Al, who lives in a field. Yes, readers, a field! Admittedly, he has a shelter to sleep in – a small, wooden hut that he built himself. But pretty much everything else, such as cooking and washing, for example, he does outdoors. I'm sure Al wouldn't mind me saying this, but as accommodations go, it's *pretty* basic.

Now, I don't know about you, readers, but I take a shower every day, and I like being able to wash my clothes once in a while, so for me, this was a new experience. To start, there was very little hot water. Al, who somehow always manages to look very clean, washes in a solar-powered outdoor shower, but last week, there wasn't enough sun to make the water really warm. Halfway through the week,

I considered the shower option, but having tested the temperature with my hand, I decided, instead, to take advantage of the facilities in the local sports center. (I know, I know!)

However, I have to say that, overall, I really enjoyed the experience of living closer to nature. I loved hearing the birds sing as I chopped vegetables for dinner in the outdoor kitchen. Reading my book on what Al calls his "roof terrace" – the very strong (!) roof of his hut, I felt more relaxed than I can remember feeling for ages. And at night, in the hut, which Al very kindly let me stay in while he slept under the stars, I had, by far, the best sleep I've had in years.

You've probably noticed that I haven't mentioned the bathroom facilities. Perhaps that's for the best!

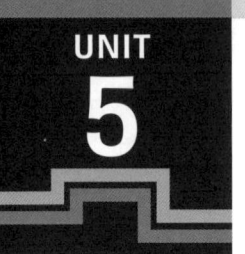

Money and shopping

5A — LANGUAGE

GRAMMAR: Zero and first conditional; future time clauses

1 Complete the sentences with the verbs in the box.

> don't work   work   won't work   works
> will pay   pay   pays   won't pay

1 I'll cut the grass every week if you _____ me.

2 We get seven dollars for each kilo of fruit we pick. If you _____ hard, you can earn a lot.

3 Rafi can have the watch as soon as she _____ me for it.

4 If Alex doesn't offer us enough cash, we _____ for him.

5 Anna won't pass her exams unless she _____ harder.

6 If Marco isn't prepared to do as much as his colleagues, we _____ him.

7 We have no other choice. If we _____ , we don't eat – it's that simple!

8 If they finish the job by the end of the day, I _____ them extra.

2 Use the prompts to complete zero or first conditionals or future time clauses. Include commas where necessary.

1 I _____ me to. (not call you/again today/unless/want)

2 If you _____ you one. (not have/raincoat/I/lend)

3 Ed's so shy. If you _____ bright red. (try/speak to him/usually/go)

4 Your hands _____ gloves. (get cold/if/not wear)

5 You've broken Rick's guitar! He _____ ! (be/really angry/when/find out)

6 Mom _____ my room. (not let/me/go out/until/clean)

VOCABULARY: Money

3 Match the <u>underlined</u> words with the words in the box.

> mortgage   bill   cash   loan   taxes   coin   broke   wealthy

1 I do some jobs for my neighbor, and he pays me in <u>paper and metal money</u>. _____

2 She must be <u>rich – she has three houses</u>. _____

3 You have to put a <u>piece of metal money</u> into the machine to make it work. _____

4 I want to buy a new car, so I'm going to ask the bank for a <u>sum of money I have to pay back</u>. _____

5 He couldn't go to the restaurant because he was completely <u>without any money</u>. _____

6 Do you think that rich people should pay more <u>money that goes to the government</u>? _____

7 Half of their wages go to paying the <u>money they owe the bank for their house</u>. _____

8 Inside the card was a $50 <u>piece of paper money</u>. _____

4 Complete the second sentence to mean the same as the first.

1 Eva let Kris have $15 until Friday.
   Eva _____ Kris $15 until Friday.

2 Petra got $30 from the ATM.
   Petra _____ out $30 from the ATM.

3 Rochelle bought us each a pizza.
   Rochelle _____ for our pizzas.

4 Peter lent Ollie the train fare.
   Ollie _____ the train fare from Peter.

5 Clara gave Wes the money she owed him.
   Clara _____ Wes back.

6 Janie bought the jacket with her credit card.
   Janie _____ for the jacket by credit card.

7 Yolanda deposited the money into her savings account.
   Yolanda _____ the money into her savings account.

PRONUNCIATION: Intonation

5 ▶ 5.1 Listen and repeat the sentences. Pay attention to the falling intonation.

1 If John and I go out, it's usually to the theater.

2 We'll be late if you don't hurry.

3 I won't go to the show unless Kate wants to.

4 If it's too warm, I'll open the window.

5 Molly gets angry if we tease her.

6 I'll talk to Dan if I see him.

READING: Identifying opinions

Buy Nothing Day

A Did you know that next Saturday is international "Buy Nothing Day"? No, me neither until an email from an anti-consumerist group popped into my inbox yesterday. Apparently, the idea is that we should all keep our cash firmly in our pockets for one day, just to show the big corporations that they don't control us completely.

B I went out to the mall in downtown Santiago, to see what shoppers there think of the idea. First, I met Camila, a 20-year-old student, struggling with armloads of new purchases. "As far as I'm concerned, the whole idea sounds a bit ridiculous," she told me. "If I don't go shopping this Saturday, I'll just buy even more next week instead."

C Javier, who works in a phone store, disagrees. "If you ask me, we all consume far too much, and we could benefit from stopping, even for just one day. Campaigns like this could be a useful way of making people more aware of their own actions. Too many people are making themselves miserable by wasting money on stuff they don't even need."

D Tamara, eighteen, was the only person I spoke to who had actually heard of Buy Nothing Day. "I took part in something called a 'zombie walk' last year," she told me. "The idea was that advertising kills people's brains and turns them into the living dead – like zombies! We all walked around a department store dressed up like dead people, getting in everyone else's way." And does she have similar plans this year? "To be honest, I don't think it was that effective. The same people are organizing a mass credit card cut-up, but I won't be taking part."

E Camila looks at Tamara in amazement. "Cutting up my credit card would be like cutting off a hand for me!" she laughs. "I can't see how anyone lives without one." "I wish more people would cut up their cards," Javier says quietly. "It seems to me that we're so busy worrying about whether we have the smartest clothes or the newest phones, we forget about the important things in life, like friends and family and culture." He stops and laughs, "But please don't tell my boss I said that!"

1 Read the text quickly. Are the statements true or false?

1 Most of the young people in the text like the idea of Buy Nothing Day. _____

2 The "zombie walk" expresses a similar idea to Buy Nothing Day. _____

3 Javier's boss would be pleased to support Buy Nothing Day. _____

2 Read the text again and decide who has the following opinions. Write C for Camila, J for Javier, T for Tamara, or N if nobody expresses the opinion.

1 Buy Nothing Day is a silly idea. _____

2 Companies' profits go down on Buy Nothing Day. _____

3 It would be good for everyone to buy less. _____

4 Events like Buy Nothing Day can make people think about their behavior. _____

5 People often get into debt because they buy too much. _____

6 Shoppers become unhappy when they buy goods that are unnecessary. _____

7 The zombie walk wasn't very effective. _____

8 It is necessary for most people to have a credit card. _____

9 Destroying your credit card is a good idea. _____

10 We place too much importance on buying things. _____

3 Complete each sentence with *even* or *just*. Then match the uses of *even* and *just* with meanings a–f.

1 You need to wait here _____ for one minute.

2 George earns a lot, but his brother is _____ more wealthy. _____

3 Katie took my bike, and she didn't _____ ask. _____

4 We all managed to climb the mountain – _____ Rod! _____

5 This jacket is _____ what I need for winter. _____

6 To get a cup of coffee, you _____ press this button. _____

a expressing surprise

b *exactly*

c *simply*

d *only*

e emphasizing a negative

f emphasizing a comparison

GRAMMAR: Predictions: *will, be going to, may/might*

1 Read the sentences and match statements 1–6 with meanings a–f.

1 It's impossible for Ava to get more points than the leader now. _____
2 Ava's doing better than I expected now. _____
3 There's only one more round, and Ava's well ahead of the other competitors. _____
4 Ava will be competing against more skilled and more experienced people. _____
5 Ava's great, but there's one other competitor who's as good as her. _____
6 I can't think of anyone who's better than Ava. _____

a She might win the competition.
b She probably won't win the competition.
c She might not win the competition.
d She's not going to win the competition.
e I'm sure she'll win the competition.
f She looks like she's going to win the competition.

2 Complete the conversation with *will/won't, going to,* or *might* and verbs from the box. There may be more than one answer.

> write   enjoy   be (x 5)   have   send

A Everyone's worked so hard on next Friday's concert. It's definitely [1]_____ the best one ever!
B That's great news!
A In fact, we've sold so many tickets, I'm worried that we [2]_____ enough space.
B Do you think Rex Brown [3]_____ a review for the local paper?
A I hope so. And we've also had an enthusiastic e-mail from a music magazine, so I think they [4]_____ a journalist, too.
B I hope you [5]_____ too nervous on the night of the concert.
A I don't think it [6]_____ too bad because everyone in the audience [7]_____ a fan.
B I wish I wasn't working that night. But if I leave early I [8]_____ able to see the second half.
A Please try to come. I'm sure you [9]_____ it!

VOCABULARY: Shopping

3 Complete the sentences with the words and phrases in the box.

> salesclerk   sold out   in-store   checkout
> reasonable   sale   in stock

1 If something is _____, it is available to buy immediately.
2 The job of a _____ is to serve customers in a store.
3 If the price of a product is _____, it is worth at least as much as you paid for it.
4 When products are being sold for less than usual, they are on _____.
5 When there is no more left to buy of a product, it is _____.
6 _____ shopping is done in a store rather than online.
7 The place where you pay for your shopping is the _____.

4 Complete the conversation with shopping words.

Zack Going shopping is so tiring! It's much easier to sit in an armchair and [1]b_____ loads of different websites.
Harvey But I much prefer to see things before I buy them.
Zack That's why I usually [2]o_____ a few things and choose the best one.
Harvey But then you have to [3]r_____ the ones you don't want – I just can't be bothered! And I think online shopping encourages people to buy too much. It's too easy to put lots of [4]i_____ in your [5]b_____. In a store, you know you're going to have to carry them home, and it feels more real.
Zack But I think online shopping actually saves you money. You can check the price of a [6]p_____ on different sites to make sure you get the best deal.
Harvey The other important thing for me is that once I've bought something, I can have it immediately – I don't like waiting!
Zack Yeah, but lots of sites have free next-day [7]d_____, and you don't have to carry anything home!

PRONUNCIATION: Word stress

5 ▶5.2 Read the sentences aloud. Remember to pronounce *probably* with two syllables and *definitely* with three syllables. Listen and repeat.

1 She probably won't answer.
2 The weather will probably get better.
3 You'll definitely pass your exams.
4 Becky is probably going to come later.
5 Dad definitely won't be happy.
6 It's definitely not going to snow.

SPEAKING: Explaining what's wrong

1 ▶ 5.3 Gisela works in a clothing store. Listen to her conversations with two customers and complete the sentences.

1 The woman's T-shirt doesn't _____. It's too _____.

2 Gisela offers her a smaller _____.

3 The woman asks for a _____.

4 She doesn't have the _____.

5 She agrees to _____ it for a smaller T-shirt.

6 The second customer would like to _____ a coat.

7 The coat is _____ on the inside.

8 He has changed his mind about the coat and doesn't _____ it any more.

2 Match items a–e with problems 1–5.

1 It's scratched. _____

2 It keeps crashing. _____

3 There's something wrong with the back wheel. _____

4 It's too tight. _____

5 There are some pieces missing. _____

a jigsaw

b tablet

c CD

d shirt

e bicycle

3 Complete the conversation with the words in the box. There are three extra words.

work   possible   missing   broken   could
exchange   wrong   return   like   model

A Can I help you, sir?

B ¹_____ I ²_____ this camera, please?

A Is there a problem with it, sir?

B Yes. It doesn't ³_____.

A Not at all?

B No. I can't even get it to turn on. I think there's something ⁴_____ with the "on" button.

A May I look? Oh yes, I think it's ⁵_____. I'll get you another one.

B I think I'd ⁶_____ a refund, if that's ⁷_____.

A Certainly, sir.

4 For 1–6, use your own ideas to explain what is wrong or to say what you would like to happen. Do not use the same phrase twice.

1 I'm returning these headphones.

_____

Could I exchange them for another pair, please?

2 I'd like to return this jacket. It's too big.

_____

3 Could I return this video game?

_____

I'd like another one, if that's possible.

4 I'd like to return this flashlight. It's broken.

_____

5 I bought this printer last week, and it doesn't work.

_____

6 I'd like to exchange these pants, please.

_____

HOME   BLOG   **PODCASTS**   ABOUT   CONTACT

Learning Curve

Tom and Sam talk about house sharing.

LISTENING

1 ▶ 5.4 Listen to the podcast and check (✔) the correct sentences.

a James said he didn't have any money. _____

b Jessica and her roommate always refused to lend James any money. _____

c Jessica and her roommate often gave James money. _____

d Jessica and her roommate told James's parents about the problem. _____

e In the end, James gave Jessica and her roommate the money he owed them. _____

2 ▶ 5.4 Listen again and complete the sentences with one or two words.

1 Sam gives an example of a mean roommate who argues about the gas or _____.

2 Tom complains that Sam never buys the _____.

3 Jessica shared a house with two other people when she was in _____.

4 Jessica and her roommate often _____ James money, but he didn't pay them back.

5 Jessica used to feel guilty when she saw that James had nothing _____.

6 James's parents were _____.

7 Jessica told James that she would _____ his parents.

8 Jessica thinks that James asked someone for a _____ so that he could pay back the money he owed.

READING

1 Read Kate's blog on page 31 and choose the best summary.

Kate wants to

a stop wasting her money on products that she does not need.

b spend less so that she can save enough money for a vacation.

c buy nothing during the month of January.

2 Choose the correct options to complete the sentences.

1 Kate thinks that the people who read her blog
   a won't believe she can change her spending habits.
   b will think that it will be easy for her to change her spending habits.
   c will try to help her change her spending habits.

2 Kate's goal is to
   a get Simon's permission before she buys anything.
   b have enough money for an exciting vacation abroad.
   c only buy things that cost less than $30.

3 Simon will help Kate by
   a always going shopping with her.
   b giving her advice about what she should and should not buy.
   c stopping her from buying anything.

4 According to Kate, 30 percent of people who shop using their cell phone
   a buy sports gear.
   b do this while they are at the doctor's.
   c do this while they are waiting.

5 It is clear that Simon has told Kate
   a to send some unnecessary items back to the company.
   b never to buy yoga pants.
   c not to use her cell phone to shop.

6 When Kate tries on clothes, she
   a never thinks she looks nice in the mirror.
   b thinks she always looks fantastic.
   c always takes advice from the staff in the store.

HOME   BLOG   PODCASTS   ABOUT   CONTACT

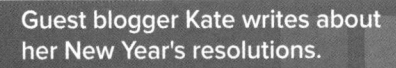

Guest blogger Kate writes about her New Year's resolutions.

My January goals

OK, I'm a week or so late with these, but better late than never! As it's the time of year for New Year's resolutions, I've decided to make a fresh start with my finances. Yes, friends, it may be a huge challenge for someone like me, but I'm going to try to change the spending habits of a lifetime! (Now, don't look at me like that – I'll become a saver, not a spender – you'll see!) And **here's how:** I now have a "money buddy." His name is Simon, and this is how it works. I've told Simon about my aim for this year – to save up enough money to go skydiving in the summer in Lake Wanaka, New Zealand. Simon and I have agreed that if I want to buy a big item, I'll ask him first. Simply, I won't buy anything costing over $30 unless he says I can. Those of you who have met Simon know that he's pretty strict, so he should be good in this role! (He's already made me return some shoes that I bought in December.☹)

No more browsing while waiting! Now, I'm clearly not alone in this habit. Apparently, 30 percent of people who use their cell phones to shop do so while waiting in line. This is a habit that I'm *totally* going to break. *This month*! No more browsing

sports gear while I'm in the doctor's waiting room because we all know what happens when I do that … (And, yes, Simon, I'm returning those two pairs of yoga pants that I don't need. They're in the mail right now, on their way back to the company.)

No visiting the shopping malls. At least when I order something online, there's no salesclerk to tell me that I look fantastic in whatever piece of clothing I'm trying on! (And I'm the kind of person who believes what the salesclerks say, even when the mirror tells a different story!)

No taking advantage of discounts, even when they seem amazing. And for anyone else who struggles when items are on sale, let me pass on my money buddy's words of wisdom: "If you don't *need* something, you're wasting your money when you buy, it *whatever* the price."

If I do all these things, I'll definitely be able to save enough money for my trip to New Zealand. So wish me luck, readers, and I'll check in next month to let you know how I'm doing.

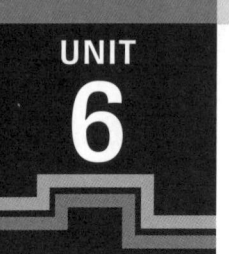

UNIT 6
Work and education

6A | LANGUAGE

GRAMMAR: Present perfect and simple past, *already*, *yet*, *recently*

1 Complete the sentences with the verbs in the box.

> have you done   have lived   went
> hasn't been   did you do
> didn't go   lived   has been

1 Vicky _____ to Buenos Aires twice this year.

2 _____ your homework yet?

3 I wonder why Laura _____ to see us recently?

4 Carol and Dom's house is in Barcelona. They _____ in Spain for several years now.

5 When he was a child, Rory _____ with his grandparents.

6 Jake _____ to Tokyo for two weeks last spring.

7 _____ any surfing while you were in Australia?

8 Rose _____ to Owen's party last weekend.

2 Complete the text with the present perfect or simple past form of the verbs in parentheses.

> My father ¹_____ (work) in Kenya for five years when I was a child, and we all went with him. My parents ²_____ (be) back every two years since then, but since I ³_____ (start) work three years ago, I ⁴_____ (not be) able to go with them. Unfortunately, I'm not free when they're going this year either, so I ⁵_____ (decide) to go on my own.
> I still have a couple of good friends in Nairobi, and although I ⁶_____ (not see) them for a few years, we keep in touch by e-mail and Skype. I ⁷_____ (get) a wonderful letter from one of them last week, offering to take me to Nairobi National Park. I'm really excited because I ⁸_____ (never be) there before.

VOCABULARY: Work and careers (1)

3 Match sentences 1–7 with a–g.

1 They gave Ravi a better job with more money. _____

2 Hamza spent a week away from the office learning how to design a website. _____

3 When Aidan was 65, he stopped working. _____

4 Jack worked for an electronics company as part of his degree. _____

5 Rick's job wasn't needed any more, and he had to leave the company. _____

6 Ivan worked at a local newspaper before he applied for a job with a national paper. _____

7 Alex decided to leave his job. _____

a He took a training course.
b He did a job placement.
c He resigned.
d He retired.
e He got experience first.
f He got a promotion.
g He was laid off.

4 Complete the words for work and careers.

1 Now I've got so much experience, I deserve to get a p_____.

2 Ayesha got f_____ for doing online shopping at work.

3 I'm going to college to get the s_____ I need to become a translator.

4 Do you believe that politicians who lie should r_____?

5 Paloma managed to get an i_____ with a fashion magazine during her summer vacation.

6 I need to earn some cash. Where's the best place to l_____ for a job?

PRONUNCIATION: Present perfect and simple past

5 ▶ 6.1 Listen and complete the sentences with verbs in the present perfect or simple past. Then listen again and repeat.

1 I _____ Ethan to come to the meeting.

2 David _____ to Mexico last year.

3 They _____ a horse.

4 I _____ my friend to help me.

5 Did you know that Scott _____ to Chicago?

6 They _____ a new car.

LISTENING: Understanding specific information

1 Before you listen to the conversation about Megan's future education, match questions 1–10 with the information you need (a–j).

1 What is Sue Kerridge's job? ....
2 What is Megan's dad's name? ....
3 How does Megan feel about school? ....
4 Why does her dad want her to go to college? ....
5 How much more can people with college degrees earn? ....
6 What does Megan enjoy doing when she needs to? ....
7 What does Sue suggest Megan should do before she decides about her future? ....
8 What sort of engineering company does she mention, in particular? ....
9 Do people doing internships usually earn more than people with a normal job? ....
10 What does Megan think of Sue's suggestion? ....

   a an amount of money
   b a word that shows an emotion
   c a piece of advice
   d a reason for something
   e the name of a job
   f an opinion
   g a comparison
   h an activity
   i a person's name
   j a type of company

2 ▶ **6.2** Listen to the conversation. Complete these answers to exercise 1.

1 She's a _____ _____.
2 _____ Dri........ .
3 She _____ it.
4 In order to have a rewarding _____.
5 An extra _____.
6 She fixes her own _____.
7 She suggests an _____ with an _____ company.
8 An _____ engineering company.
9 No, they don't usually earn as _____ as other employees.
10 She thinks it sounds _____.

3 ▶ **6.3** <u>Underline</u> the words you think will be stressed. Listen and check.

1 Going to one of the top colleges will help you get a well-paid job.
2 College isn't necessarily the best choice for everyone.
3 It's a good idea to get some work experience before you decide on a career.
4 Will wants to work as a science teacher.
5 You will need to get some more skills.
6 Some supermarkets offer training courses for future managers.

4 Complete the sentences.

1 An _____ is someone who works for someone else.
2 We usually send a _____ letter with a CV.
3 If you are _____ for something at work, you have to make sure it happens or is done.
4 Your working _____ are the circumstances that affect your job.
5 _____ jobs do not last for a fixed period of time.
6 A _____ job is one that you get satisfaction from.
7 A person who is _____ does not have a job.
8 In a _____ job, you have to do a lot of different things.

GRAMMAR: Present perfect continuous and present perfect

1 Choose the correct options to complete the sentences.

1 Ed has _____ his friend's birthday every year for the last 40 years.
   a remembered   b been remembering

2 How long have you _____ studying today?
   a been   b been spending

3 Gaby has _____ the house all morning.
   a cleaned   b been cleaning

4 I hope you haven't _____ very long.
   a waiting   b been waiting

5 Rex has _____ a member of this club for almost five years.
   a been   b been being

6 My parents have _____ this house since 1998.
   a owned   b been owning

7 I'm so tired – I've _____ wood for the fire.
   a chopped   b been chopping

8 What has Marta _____? She's covered in mud!
   a done   b been doing

2 Complete the conversation with the verbs in the box. Use the present perfect continuous or present perfect form.

> practice   know   mean   have
> take   not learn   play

Federika Hey, Adam! Is that your guitar? I didn't know you played.

Adam Well I ¹_____ for very long, and I'm not very good yet. You have a guitar, too, don't you?

Federika Yes, I do. I ²_____ it since I was four. In fact, my band has a concert next week – do you want to come?

Adam Sure, I'd love to. Are you nervous about playing?

Federika A bit. I ³_____ for weeks, but some of the songs are really difficult, and I'm still getting used to my new guitar. I ⁴_____ it for a couple of months now, but it still feels strange. By the way, do you have a teacher?

Adam Well, I ⁵_____ classes with a man my sister recommended, but I don't like him that much. Do you know anyone good?

Federika You should try Fergus Jones. I ⁶_____ him for years, and he's great. In fact, I'll call him for you if you'd like – I ⁷_____ to get in touch with him for ages.

VOCABULARY: Education

3 Read the sentences and check (✔) True or False.

1	Students usually have to pay to go to a public school.	True	False
2	A term is a period of time when students are in school.	True	False
3	You become a graduate when you start studying at a college.	True	False
4	Principals teach the oldest children in a school.	True	False
5	If you cheat on an exam, you do something that is not allowed.	True	False
6	"Taking notes" means getting written information from your teacher.	True	False
7	If you hand in work, you give it to your teacher.	True	False
8	Students are likely to get into trouble if they don't do their homework.	True	False
9	A schedule is a list of school dates, but not times.	True	False
10	Children usually start elementary school when they are 16.	True	False

4 Complete the sentences with education words.

1 The students behave in Mr. Gallagher's class. They have to, because he is very s_____.

2 My girlfriend teaches politics in college. She's a l_____.

3 Lola isn't at home during the semester because she goes to b_____ s_____.

4 Gustavo's at the University of São Paulo doing a d_____ in Engineering.

5 Samira's studying in the library because she has to r_____ her notes for an important exam.

6 Anna's daughter is three, so she just started n_____ s_____.

7 Ian's parents saved all their money in order to send him to a p_____ s_____.

8 Ben worked really hard on his essay, and his teacher gave him a g_____ g_____.

9 Astrid had to take her exams again because she f_____ them the first time.

10 We get our g_____ next week – I'm so nervous because I need to pass this course!

PRONUNCIATION: Weak form of *been*

5 ▶ 6.4 Listen and repeat. Pay attention to the pronunciation of *been* and the way the words are stressed.

1 She hasn't been married for long.

2 I've been hoping to meet her.

3 The children have been playing.

4 Have you been talking to Luca?

5 Veronica's been complaining again.

6 Kyle's been having problems at work.

WRITING: Writing a cover letter

SUMMER CAMP COUNSELORS NEEDED FOR LANGUAGE SCHOOL

Sunshine School provides summer camps for over 1,000 teenagers from around the world. We aim to develop their language skills in a comfortable, safe, but fun environment.

Counselors' duties include:
- organizing sports and art activities
- accompanying students on cultural visits
- supervising meal times

Candidates should:
- be reliable and friendly
- work well as part of a team
- be energetic and enthusiastic
- have excellent written and spoken English

A knowledge of one or more foreign languages and good IT skills would be an advantage.

To apply, please send your CV to David Green, explaining why you are interested in this position. Please provide details of your qualifications, skills, and any relevant experience.

1 Read Lulu's cover letter. Complete 1–11 with the correct prepositions.

○ ○ ○

Dear Mr. Green,

I am writing to apply ^1_____ the position of Summer Camp Counselor. <u>My CV's attached to this e-mail.</u> I am currently doing a degree ^2_____ psychology. I am particularly interested ^3_____ working with young people in the future, so I believe that working ^4_____ a summer camp counselor would be the ideal job for me.
I am passionate ^5_____ travel and language learning because they help people from different countries understand each other. I am proficient ^6_____ Spanish and Russian, and <u>I'm trying to learn Japanese at the moment.</u> I believe that my knowledge of languages would help me communicate well with your students.
Last year, I had a summer job with the city youth program. I enjoyed working as part of a group that was responsible ^7_____ sports activities. I worked with children from different backgrounds and helped to support children who found group activities difficult. <u>It was wonderful!</u> In addition, I babysat once a week, which shows that I am a reliable person. <u>I have loads of energy, and I love working with other people.</u> I believe that this, together with my experience, makes me ideal ^8_____ the role, and I would very much welcome the opportunity to work ^9_____ your organization.
Thank you ^10_____ considering my application.
I look forward ^11_____ hearing from you.

<u>All the best,</u>
Lulu Ramirez

2 Check (✔) the points from the job ad that Lulu includes in her letter.

1 organizing sports activities _____
2 organizing art activities _____
3 accompanying students on cultural visits _____
4 supervising meal times _____
5 being reliable _____
6 being friendly _____
7 working well as part of a team _____
8 being energetic _____
9 being enthusiastic _____
10 having excellent written and spoken English _____
11 knowing other languages _____
12 having good IT skills _____

3 Rewrite the <u>underlined</u> sentences from Lulu's cover letter in a more formal style.

1 My CV's attached to this e-mail.

_____

2 I'm trying to learn Japanese at the moment.

_____

3 It was wonderful!

_____

4 I've got loads of energy, and I love working with other people.

_____

5 All the best,

_____

4 The same school is looking for someone to arrange transportation from the airport for adult students arriving in the U.S. during July and August.

Read the job description below and write a cover letter to David Green, applying for that job. Remember to provide details of your qualifications, skills, and any relevant experience.

Duties include:
- reserving buses and cabs to meet students at U.S. airports
- contacting host families to arrange accommodations for students

Candidates should:
- have a good level of education
- have a polite, confident telephone manner
- be extremely well-organized and reliable
- be prepared to work on weekends

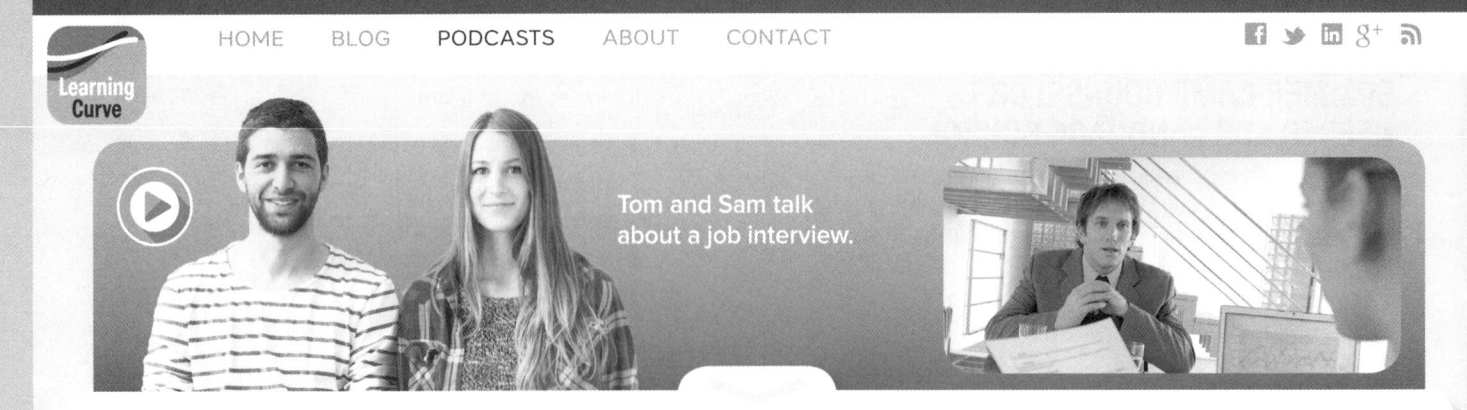

HOME   BLOG   **PODCASTS**   ABOUT   CONTACT

Learning Curve

Tom and Sam talk about a job interview.

LISTENING

1 ▶ **6.5** Listen to the podcast and check (✔) the words that you hear.

a varied   _____
b stressful   _____
c skills   _____
d well-paid   _____
e rewarding   _____
f career   _____
g application form _____
h part-time   _____
i full-time   _____
j permanent   _____

2 ▶ **6.5** Listen again and choose the correct options to complete the sentences.

1 After an interview, Tom once accidentally
   a started a fire.
   b made an alarm start.
   c broke a window.

2 Patrick has been trying to find a new job for
   a eighteen months.
   b twelve months.
   c six months.

3 Patrick has had his present job for about
   a half a year.
   b three years.
   c three and a half years.

4 Patrick's friend
   a used to work for the computer company.
   b started working for the company five years ago.
   c has applied for the same job as Patrick.

5 During the interview, Patrick noticed that
   a the man was reading his application form.
   b the woman was reading his application form.
   c both interviewers were reading his application form.

6 Patrick explained that he wasn't applying for
   a a full-time job.
   b a permanent job.
   c the position of telephone sales representative.

READING

1 Read Jack's blog on page 37 and choose the best summary.

a College is not the best way to get a good job.
b You need work experience to get a good job.
c College is not the only way to get a good job.

2 Check (✔) the correct sentences.

1 Jack is very happy for the young people who are going to go to college. _____

2 Jack says that you do not need a college degree to get a good job. _____

3 Will studied at a public school. _____

4 Will always listened carefully during his classes. _____

5 Will didn't get any experience cooking on his first job in a restaurant. _____

6 All of the restaurants that Will worked in were successful. _____

7 In one of his jobs, Will had to do the same task all the time. _____

8 One of Will's bosses realized that he was talented and gave him a more important job. _____

3 Use words and phrases from the blog to complete sentences 1–6.

1 My father was very depressed after he was _____ _____.

2 If I _____ _____ _____, I will earn more money.

3 My son got excellent _____, so we went to a restaurant to celebrate.

4 I took a _____ to learn new skills.

5 I wanted to _____ _____ of work before I finished college, so I always got a job during the summer.

6 I got my _____ in history, so I became a history teacher.

HOME **BLOG** PODCASTS ABOUT CONTACT

Guest blogger Jack talks about alternatives to college.

Where there's a Will ...

During the next few weeks, young people across the country will graduate from high school. Some will spend the next four years getting a degree in college. Congratulations to those bright young people! I know how hard they've all been working for the last several years. I hope they've gotten the grades they need to continue with their education and sincerely wish them all the best with their studies.

However, I think it's worth reminding any young readers out there that a college education isn't the *only* route to a successful career.

Take my business partner, Will, for example. Will was sixteen when he left school. (This was allowed in his state!) His parents had sent him to an expensive private school where the poor guy kept getting into trouble for not paying attention in class. He wasn't a *bad boy*, you understand – I mean he never misbehaved really badly or did anything terrible. He just wasn't very interested in the subjects that he was being taught. (Probably rather disappointing for his poor parents who, I'm sure, only wanted the best for him!)

However, there was one topic that Will was *extremely* interested in learning about when he was a teenager – one thing that he was prepared to work *really hard* at. And that topic was FOOD. For as long as he can remember, he's loved cooking (and of course eating!). When the other boys were kicking a ball around in the park, Will was in the kitchen, looking through his mom's recipe books (or, when she allowed it, cooking!). As soon as he was old enough, he got a weekend job, washing dishes in a restaurant, just so that he could experience a professional kitchen. While his classmates were studying for exams, Will was busy loading plates into huge, industrial dishwashers. He's worked in a kitchen ever since.

Will's career path has twisted and turned – that's to be expected. The work has been exhausting – and, no doubt, stressful. In the early years, he was laid off several times because the restaurants he was working in weren't making enough money. At one stage, he was holding two part-time jobs, just to earn enough money. In another job, he spent ten hours a day, six days a week, preparing vegetables. But after a year in that job, his manager recognized his ability (or at least his enthusiasm!), and he got a promotion. And all this time, he was learning new skills and getting valuable experience.

Will didn't get a formal degree – in fact, he's never even taken a training course – but last year, he and I finally bought our own restaurant together. Congratulations, Will – I'm so proud of you!

WRITING: Making a narrative interesting

I have a really good friend named Jon. We don't get together very often because he's a doctor, and he works very long hours. We usually keep in touch on social media, but one Thursday evening, just before I went to bed, I got a text message. It was Jon. He wanted to invite me to dinner "next Saturday."
I replied to his text immediately and accepted his invitation. I was looking forward to seeing Jon because he's
¹_____ guy, and we have great conversations. He's also ²_____ – he always makes me laugh so hard.

On Saturday evening, I rode my bike over to his place. The weather was ³_____ – heavy rain and
⁴_____, and I couldn't wait to be in Jon's ⁵_____ living room. As soon as I arrived, I knew something was wrong. The windows of his house were dark, and when I rang the doorbell, nobody answered.
I ⁶_____.

Jon was usually very reliable, so I thought that something bad had happened to him.

I got out my phone and texted him. There was no answer. There was nothing else I could do, so I decided to go home and wait until he replied. I spent most of the evening ⁷_____ checking my phone. After more than three hours, my phone rang. It was Jon. I ⁸_____ picked up my phone and asked him if he was all right. "Why did you think I wasn't OK?" he asked in a ⁹_____. "You invited me for dinner!" I said, a little ¹⁰_____ by now.
Jon was ¹¹_____. "I invited you *next* Saturday, not *this* Saturday," he insisted.

Then we realized what the problem was. By "next Saturday" I thought he meant in two days, but what he really meant was in just over a week. We ¹²_____ with our plans in the future!

1 Read the blog post about a time when there was a communication problem and complete 1–12 with the words and phrases in the box.

> warm, cozy   terrible   eagerly   a really interesting   anxiously   amazed   puzzled voice
> have to be more careful   felt really worried   extremely amusing   very strong winds   annoyed

2 Which of 1–12 in exercise 1 match these features?

a descriptions of people _____ _____

b descriptions of places _____

c descriptions of the weather _____ _____

d descriptions of emotions and feelings
_____ _____ _____ _____ _____ _____

e a comment on the events _____

3 <u>Underline</u> all the examples of *before*, *after*, *until*, and *as soon as* in the blog and read the sentences. Then choose the correct options to complete these sentences.

1 Please reply to this e-mail _____ you have finished reading it.
a as soon as   b before   c until

2 Think very carefully _____ sharing photos on social media.
a after   b until   c before

3 I won't know the time of the meeting _____ I get an e-mail from the organizer.
a after   b until   c as soon as

4 _____ I had replied to Laura's text message, I realized I had given her the wrong number.
a After   b Until   c Before

5 I kept in touch with Boris _____ 2010, when he moved abroad, and I lost his address.
a after   b before   c until

6 I'll send you more information _____ I can go online.
a until   b before   c as soon as

7 _____ our phone call, I invited her to my office so that we could speak face to face.
a As soon as   b Until   c After

8 I need to make sure I know all the facts _____ I give my boss a call.
a before   b as soon as   c after

4 Write a blog post about a time when there was a communication problem. Use the chart to plan some words and phrases to make your narrative interesting. Use different narrative tenses and time linkers.

descriptions of people, places, and events	
descriptions of emotions and feelings	
comments about the events	

WRITING: Writing an informal e-mail

○ ○ ○

[1]Dear Katie,

(A) [2]It was a real pleasure to receive your e-mail. [3]I apologize for taking so long to reply. I've been really busy, but I'm so pleased to hear that you've managed to make up with Amy. I know she's one of your closest friends, and it's horrible having a falling out with people.

(B) Did I tell you that I got on the college soccer team? [4]It is very enjoyable, but we have to work extremely hard! We train twice a week, and there are games every weekend, all over the country. We even played in Montreal last month. It was an amazing trip! We won 3–0, and I scored two of the goals! I get along really well with all the other girls on the team. We have a lot of fun together – not just when we're playing soccer.

(C) So, are you still coming camping with us in August? I have a big tent if you want to share. I really hope you can come. [5]I am very much looking forward to seeing you. Did I tell you that Don's coming as well? You two have a lot in common – he's a big rock fan, too, so at least you'll have something to talk about!

(D) By the way, did you hear about Jack? He's getting married! Apparently, his neighbor introduced him to her cousin and that was it – two months later, they were engaged. Incredible, isn't it?

(E) Speaking of marriage, how's your sister doing? Is her baby sleeping through the night yet? I'm definitely not going to have any children until I'm at least 35!

(F) Anyway, have to go – I have soccer training in half an hour. [6]I look forward to hearing from you.

(G) [7]Sincerely yours,

Emma

1 Read Emma's e-mail to her friend Katie. Emma's style is sometimes too formal. Rewrite the underlined phrases and sentences in a more informal style.

1 _____
2 _____
3 _____
4 _____
5 _____
6 _____
7 _____

2 Which paragraphs do the following things? Circle the words in the e-mail that show this.

1 change the subject _____ _____
2 introduce a less important subject _____
3 return to a subject _____

3 Write an informal e-mail to one of your friends, telling him/her about a new friend you have made.

Include the following:
- an informal greeting
- some opening comments
- a paragraph about your new friend, e.g. how you met, your friend's personality, the things you have in common
- a paragraph in which you change the subject to ask your friend about someone you both know
- a paragraph about a less important subject
- a paragraph in which you return to the same subject as the previous paragraph
- a reason to end the e-mail
- an informal ending

Use informal discourse markers (*Anyway, So, By the way,* and *Speaking of*) to link the paragraphs.

WRITING: Writing a cover letter

○ ○ ○

Dear Sir/Madam:

1_____ Senior Sales Representative, Electronic Goods, advertised in today's *Retail News*.

As you can see from my CV, 2_____ and a certificate in soccer coaching. However, after working in the electronic goods department of a large store when I finished college, I decided that a career in sales would be more suited to my skills and personality.

After nine months at the department store, I got my current job as a sales representative with Secure Alarms, a company that provides security systems for businesses, as well as home owners. 3_____, assessing their security needs, and making sales. To do this job, it is necessary to be highly organized and have excellent customer service skills.

4_____ I am fascinated by sound systems, and keep up to date on all the latest products and developments. In addition, I have a good knowledge of cameras and photography, as well as smartphones and personal computers.

I am a very hardworking and reliable employee, and 5_____. I would welcome the opportunity to work for a respected company like yours and, if my application is successful, I am confident that I would be a valuable addition to the team.

6_____ and I look forward to hearing from you soon.

Sincerely,

Gillian Howes

1 Read Gillian's covering letter and match blanks 1–6 with phrases a–f.

a Thank you for considering my application,

b I am extremely interested in this position because

c I am responsible for meeting with customers

d I am writing to apply for the position of

e I have a degree in physical education

f I work very well as part of a team

2 Which of these things does Gillian do in her letter?

1 use formal language to end the main part of the letter _____

2 describe her personal qualities _____

3 ask about the salary _____

4 describe her qualifications _____

5 say why she would like the job _____

6 say she is good at languages _____

7 talk about her previous work experience _____

8 say which position she is applying for _____

9 explain her career goals _____

10 describe her attitude to work _____

3 Write a cover letter for this job. Remember to use formal language and include details of your qualifications, skills, and any relevant experience.

SALESCLERK, BJ OUTDOOR SPORTS

We are looking for smart, efficient sales staff for our new downtown store. The successful candidate will have:

• at least two years' experience working in a store
• excellent written and spoken English
• recognized proficiency in math
• a genuine interest in outdoor sports, especially climbing and skiing
• a knowledge of sports equipment

You will work as part of a large team. Our stores are always busy, so you must be able to work under pressure. To apply, please send your CV and a cover letter to Kelly Bagnold. Please provide details of your qualifications, skills, and any relevant experience.

Richmond

58 St Aldates
Oxford
OX1 1ST
United Kingdom

First reprint: January 2023
Printed in China
ISBN: 978-84-668-2650-1
© Richmond / Santillana Global S.L. 2017

Publishing Director: Deborah Tricker

Publisher: Simone Foster

Media Publisher: Sue Ashcroft

Workbook Publisher: Luke Baxter

Content Developer: Stephanie Bremner

Editors: Peter Anderson, Debra Emmett, Helen Ward, Tom Hadland, Eleanor Clements, Ruth Cox, Fiona Hunt, Kate Mellersh, Fiona Hunt, Helen Wendholt

Americanization: Deborah Goldblatt

Proofreaders: Bruce Wade, Tas Cooper, Shannon Neill

Design Manager: Lorna Heaslip

Cover Design: This Ain't Rock'n'Roll, London

Design & Layout: Lorna Heaslip, Oliver Hutton, ColArt Design

Photo Researcher: Magdalena Mayo

***Learning Curve* video:** Mannic Media

Audio Production: Eastern Sky Studios

App Development: The Distance

Printing and Finishing: EGB Editora Gráfica Bernardi Ltda
Lote: 775033
Cod: 290526501

We would also like to thank the following people for their valuable contribution to writing and developing the material:
Alastair Lane, Bob McLarty, Brigit Viney, Pamela Vittorio (Video Script Writer), Belen Fernandez (App Project Manager), Eleanor Clements (App Content Creator)

We would like to thank all those who have given their kind permission to reproduce material for this book:

Illustration:
Simon Clare; Dermot Flynn c/o Dutch Uncle; Guillaume Gennet c/o Lemonade; John Goodwin; The Boy FitzHammond c/o NB Illustration; Douglas Strachan at Strachangray Creative

Photos:
J. Jaime; S. Enríquez; 123RF; ALAMY/WENN Ltd., PhotoAlto sas, AF archive, HO Images, Chronicle, BSIP SA, B Christopher, Lev Dolgachov, Morey Milbradt, Richard Levine, Kevin Su, Rob Watkins, epa european pressphoto agency b.v., cineclassico, Aflo Co. Ltd., Mark Eden, Photo Japan, REUTERS, Mark phillips, Peterforsberg, Jorge Peréz, ilpo musto, Design Pics Inc, ZUMA Press, Inc., Glasshouse Images, MBI, TGSPHOTO, CoverSpot Photography, Entertainment Pictures, Allstar Picture Library, Tewin Kijthamrongworakul, Tribune Content Agency LLC, Pictorial Press Ltd, Caryn Becker; BBC; BNPS (BOURNEMOUTH NEWS & PICTURE SERVICE)

Rachel Adams, Steve Way; GETTY IMAGES SALES SPAIN/ Photodisc/Thinkstock, Photos.com Plus, Thinkstock; GTRESONLINE; I. PREYSLER; ISTOCKPHOTO/Getty Images Sales Spain; JOHN FOXX IMAGES; REX SHUTTERSTOCK/ FOX/Genre Movies, Page Images, Sipa Press, Silverhub, Galvan/AP, Ray Tang; SHUTTERSTOCK/Rex; SHUTTERSTOCK NETHERLANDS,B.V.; SOUTHWEST NEWS; wikipedia/ Ed g2s; Michael Parsons; Pedroromero2; Neil Douglas; Rockford Register Star and rrstar.com; COAST Collective Architecture Studio; Amos Magliocco/Eric Nguyen; courtsey of Vic Armstrong; Carroll County Sheriff; Project Monsoon, School of the Art Institute of Chicago; SERIDEC PHOTOIMAGENES CD; ARCHIVO SANTILLANA; GETTY IMAGES SALES SPAIN/ Westend61; ISTOCKPHOTO; Prats i Camps; ALAMY/Photo 12, Sylvie Bouchard, Dinendra Haria, Peter Wheeler, age fotostock, travelstock44, Dave Stevenson, Moviestore collection Ltd, Jim West, Mikael Damkier,Nathaniel Noir, PURPLE MARBLES, Matthew Chattle, jaileybug,ONOKY - Photononstop, Newscast Online Limited, PJF Military Collection, Kerry Dunstone, FORGET Patrick/SAGAPHOTO.COM, Chuck Pefley; GETTY IMAGES SALES SPAIN/Thinkstock; ISTOCKPHOTO/Getty Images Sales Spain; ARCHIVO SANTILLANA

Cover Photo: iStockphoto/Getty Images Sales Spain

Texts:
p.48 Adapted from 'Fabrice Muamba: how I went from professional footballer to journalist' by Hannah Friend, Guardian Professional, 11 June 2014. Copyright Guardian News & Media Ltd 2016.

p.16 Adapted from 'Meet Steve Way - England's unlikeliest athlete for the Commonwealth Games' by Sean Ingle, theguardian.com, 31 May 2014. Copyright Guardian News & Media Ltd 2016.

We would like to thank the following reviewers for their valuable feedback which has made Personal Best possible. We extend our thanks to the many teachers and students not mentioned here.
Brad Bawtinheimer, Manuel Hidalgo, Paulo Dantas, Diana Bermúdez, Laura Gutiérrez, Hardy Griffin, Angi Conti, Christopher Morabito, Hande Kokce, Jorge Lobato, Leonardo Mercato, Mercilinda Ortiz, Wendy López